WITHDRAWN

STORES

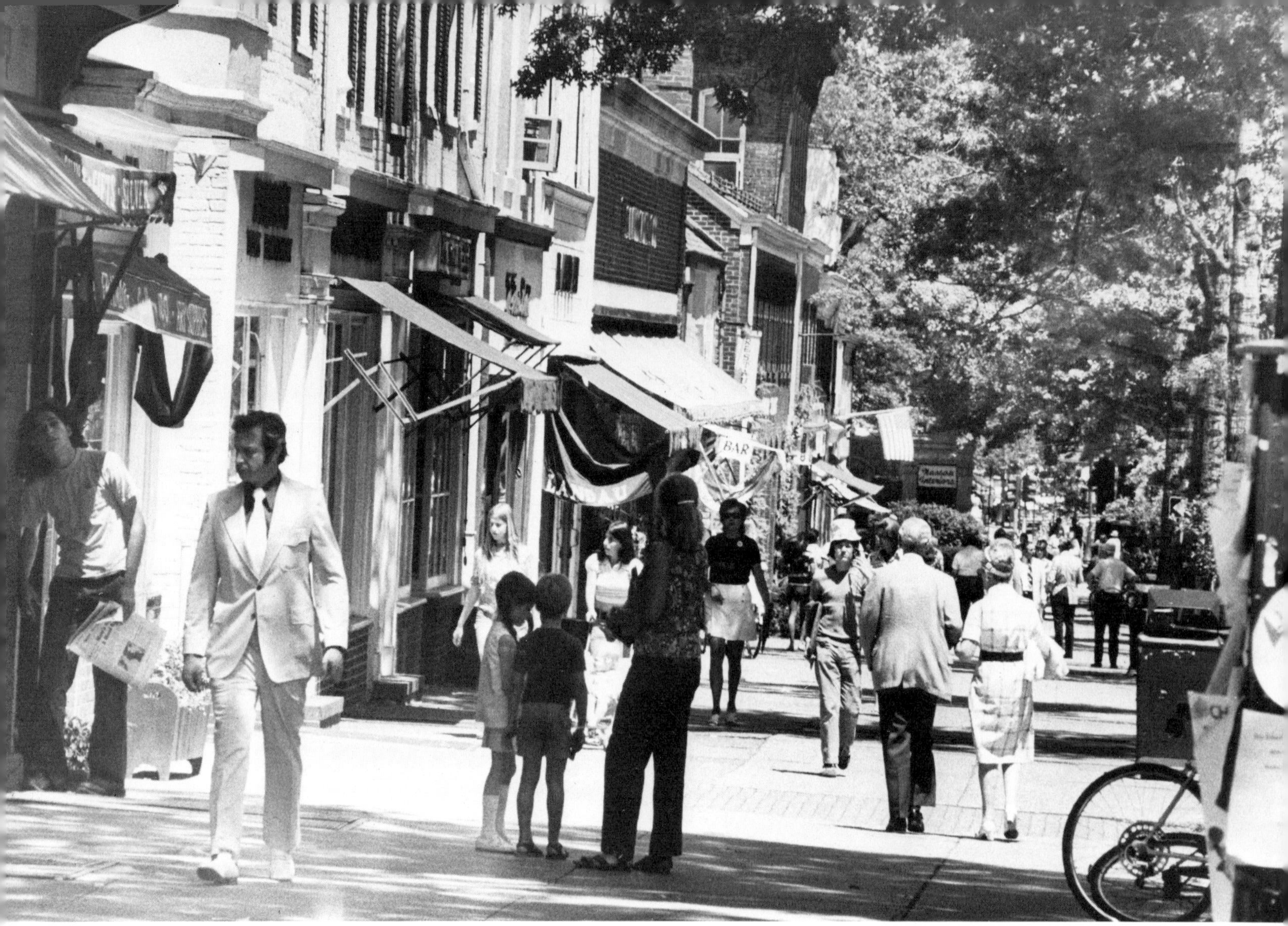
BAR

BY ALVIN SCHWARTZ
PHOTOGRAPHS BY SAMUEL NOCELLA, JR.

STORES

Macmillan Publishing Co., Inc.   New York

Copyright © 1977 Alvin Schwartz
Copyright © 1977 Macmillan Publishing Co., Inc.
All rights reserved. No part of this book may be reproduced or transmitted
in any form or by any means, electronic or mechanical, including photocopying,
recording or by any information storage and retrieval system,
without permission in writing from the Publisher.

Macmillan Publishing Co., Inc.
866 Third Avenue, New York, N.Y. 10022
Collier Macmillan Canada, Ltd.

Drawings on pages 12, 37, and 97 by Erick Ingraham
Designed by Bobye List

Printed in the United States of America
10 9 8 7 6 5 4 3 2 1

Library of Congress Cataloging in Publication Data
Schwartz, Alvin, date
   Stores.

     Includes index.
     SUMMARY: An inside look at the day-to-day
operations of forty typical stores.
     1. Stores, Retail—Juvenile literature.
2. Business—Juvenile literature. [1. Stores, Retail.
2. Business]   I. Nocella, Samuel.   II. Title.
HF5429.S357   381   76–47451
ISBN 0-02-781310-X

FOR JOHN

KEEPING STORE

In my town there are over three hundred stores. Out on the highways and in the shopping malls there are even more.

The people who live here depend on them for groceries, ice-cream cones, aspirin, diamond rings, sneakers, underwear, flower pots, light bulbs, loans when they need money, and all kinds of other things.

A few of these stores are owned by big companies that also own stores elsewhere. But most are small businesses the owners run themselves or with the help of a few relatives or employees.

Many stores in this town have been here for years. But from time to time one goes out of business or is sold to another storekeeper. A short while ago, for example, the laundromat in this book went out of business. And the bakery was sold to another baker.

To stay in business, a storekeeper must,

of course, make a profit. This means he must make enough money from what he sells to pay for his merchandise, rent, electricity, and other costs and still have enough left over to earn a living. To do so he often must charge twice as much for a product as he paid for it.

Each year nine or ten people start new stores here, but not all of them succeed. Either they do not have the products people want. Or they do not have a good location—renting a store on a main street may cost $1,000 a month or more. Or they did not realize how much work keeping store would be.

Storekeepers were the world's first businessmen. Over five thousand years ago they were making weapons or jewelry or other products. Or they grew food. Then they sold these wares in a marketplace in open stalls or on the bare ground.

Or they filled a pack or a basket and walked from place to place peddling whatever they had. Later they also moved about in wagons, which were something like stores on wheels.

But today's stores are, for the most part, in buildings, not in stalls, packs, or wagons. And today's marketplaces are business districts or shopping malls, not open fields. And they are complicated.

There is, in fact, so much for sale it confuses the eye. In a large store often there are ten thousand different products or more, most of which come from hundreds or thousands of miles away.

To keep track of what they have in stock, some merchants now use computers. Some supermarkets also use them to operate automatic checkout stations. And some banks use them to wait on customers.

But in one important way stores are no different than they ever were. We depend on them for much of what we need and much of what we want.

It is 8:30 A.M. and Urken's Hardware on Witherspoon Street has just opened for business.

But Mrs. Urken and her son Irv and the others who work here have been busy for over an hour. Each morning before the store opens, they unpack new merchandise, restock their shelves and bins, order other products they need, send bills to their customers, and pay bills of their own.

Then they sweep the floor and the sidewalk in front, set up a display of garden tools and garbage cans, and wait for customers.

At some stores the day begins even earlier.

At the Acme supermarket just outside town the day begins at midnight when four men start unpacking a small mountain of groceries, fruit, and vegetables. They stamp each item with its price and place it on the right shelf or rack or in a bin or freezer.

At the Balt Bakery, Alfred Goetz and John King begin work at 3 A.M. While almost everybody else sleeps, they bake what Mrs. Goetz will sell later today in the small shop out front. Using flour, water, milk, sugar, eggs, margarine, shortening, and yeast, they mix eight kinds of batter in this machine.

Then they turn this batter into forty loaves of bread, a thousand cookies and brownies, five hundred doughnuts, a hundred Danish pastries . . . and twenty pies and forty cakes—almost all of which will be gone when Mrs. Goetz closes up and goes home late this afternoon. Whatever is left will be sold tomorrow at a discount or given away.

At the Grotto restaurant, Mike Pilenza begins work at 6 A.M. He is not only the owner, he is the chief cook. Soon after he arrives he starts the spaghetti and the other dishes his customers will eat later in the day.

Only Wednesdays are different. Then he begins at 4 A.M., for that is the day he also must drive to a big city nearby to do his marketing.

By 8 A.M. the assistant cook is at work. So is the "pantryman," or helper, and so is the dishwasher who cleans the pots and pans they use.

Since it takes five hours to make a good spaghetti sauce, Mr. Pilenza starts with that. This morning it is a tomato sauce. He must make enough for two hundred orders of spaghetti and meatballs, since that is how much his customers usually eat each day.

First he fills a large pot with tomatoes, tomato paste, water, and spices. Then he mixes everything together with a wooden paddle, and starts it simmering, cooking it just below the boiling point.

Next he fills a roasting pan with meat bones, meat scraps, celery, and onions, adds olive oil and garlic, and bakes it in an oven at 500 degrees. When this mixture is well done, he adds it to the tomato sauce, then lets it all simmer for four hours more.

While the sauce bubbles, the assistant cook and the pantryman make meatballs.

Next they cook spaghetti noodles until they are almost done, divide them into individual portions, and store them in the refrigerator until they are needed.

Then they start to prepare the lasagna, ravioli, chicken cacciatore, veal parmigiana, and other dishes they will need.

At about 11 A.M. Mr. Pilenza gently stirs the spaghetti sauce with his paddle, removes the meat bones and meat scraps, stirs again, and tastes. Then he adds a little of this and a little of that, tastes again—and smacks his lips and smiles.

If you are having two hundred people to dinner soon, and they would like spaghetti and meatballs, Mr. Pilenza would like you to try his recipe. If you are not an expert cook, get your mother or father to help you. If you don't need two hundred servings, they can also help you make a smaller amount.

Mike Pilenza's Spaghetti and Meatballs for 200 People

12 GALLONS OF TOMATO SAUCE

Add the following ingredients to a heavy 20-gallon pot:
- 9 gallons canned crushed tomatoes
- 2 gallons tomato paste
- 3 gallons cold water
- 2 handfuls salt (Mr. Pilenza has big hands)
- 3 bay leaves
- 1 dash oregano

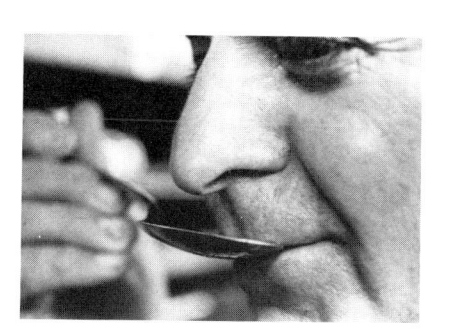

Simmer over low heat, stirring frequently. While the sauce simmers place the following ingredients in a large roasting pan:
- 10 pounds pork neck bones and veal and beef scraps
- ½ gallon olive oil
- 1 clove garlic
- 4 onions cut in quarters
- 4 stalks of celery, chopped
- 10 rosemary leaves
- 2 handfuls of salt
- 1 dash of black pepper
- 1 handful oregano
- 1 handful sweet basil

Bake for one hour at 500 degrees. Then pour the contents of the baking pan into the pot and simmer for four hours more. Strain through a large colander to remove solids.

200 BIG MEATBALLS

While the tomato sauce simmers, mix the following ingredients in a large pan:

- 20 *pounds ground meat (pork, veal and beef mixed)*
- 12 *eggs*
- 5 *pounds white bread, broken into pieces, soaked in water, squeezed dry*
- ½ *pound Romano and Parmesan cheeses, mixed and grated*
- 1 *handful salt*
- 1 *dash black pepper*
- 1 *large garlic clove cut up fine*
- 4 *tablespoons sweet basil*
- 4 *tablespoons oregano*

Shape the meatballs with an ice-cream scoop or a soup spoon and your hands. Bake at 450 degrees for 45 minutes.

SPAGHETTI NOODLES

You will need about fifty pounds. Follow the directions on the box.

When everything is ready, fill each plate or bowl with spaghetti, put a meatball on top, and cover it with a lot of tomato sauce. Then heat in the oven for another minute or two, and serve.

BER	BALANCE
5313	1,190.71
5362	1,643.27
5461	23,981.40
5545	3,906.94
5594	3,268.06
5636	959.31
5693	33,411.15
5743	646.70
5925	50.00
5966	1,091.47
6022	2,101.50
6147	34.93
6196	719.01
6238	503.04

At about the time Mr. Pilenza starts his spaghetti sauce, a machine at the First National Bank automatically starts typing a report the bank's computer prepared during the night.

The report tells how much money each of the bank's sixteen thousand customers now has in his or her checking account. When the bank opens at 9 A.M. the tellers who work there will need this information to make sure customers do not withdraw more money than they have.

By 7:30 A.M. three or four small grocery stores have opened. So has the Balt Bakery. So has the newsstand at the railroad station. So have the many gas stations people here depend on for gasoline to get to work.

This man is pumping gas at Will's service station on the Hightstown Road. Each morning probably fifty cars stop here to fill up. If you happened to be under this car and looked up, this is what you would see.

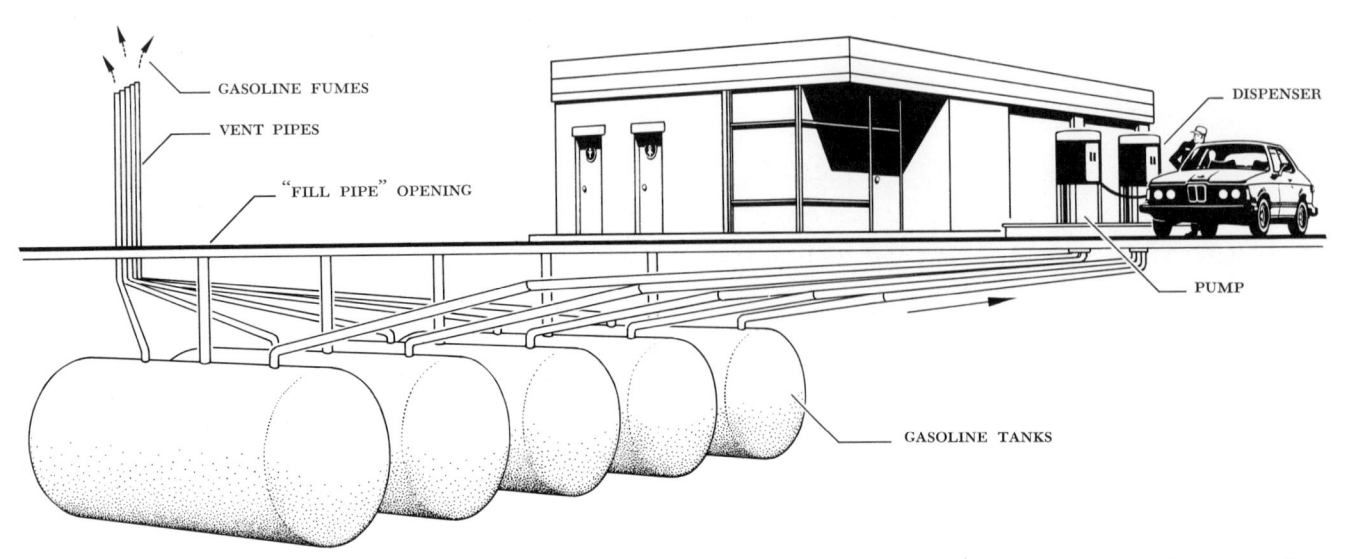

The hose the attendant is holding is really just one end of a big machine, most of which is underground. As the drawing shows, it is attached to what most people call a pump, but what actually is a "dispenser." The dispenser is attached by pipes to five big tanks buried about fifty feet away. Each holds four thousand gallons of gasoline.

When the attendant picks up the hose and squeezes a lever inside the handle, a pump down below sends a stream of gasoline from one of the tanks through a pipe . . . to the dispenser . . . through the hose . . . to the car.

Other pipes connect the tanks to vents at the back of the gas station. They carry off gasoline fumes which might explode if they collected underground.

Each day the people who work at Will's sell about two thousand gallons of gasoline. To make sure their customers can see where they are going, they also use fifteen hundred paper towels and one gallon of windshield washer.

When the big gate at the Grover Lumber Company swung open at 8 A.M. there was a line of carpenters, plumbers, electricians, masons, and other craftsmen waiting with their trucks to pick up the supplies they will need today.

These supplies include "lumber," which means boards and plywood, and "millwork," which means moldings, doors, door frames, windows, porch posts, and flooring.

They also include plaster board, insulation, cinder blocks, bricks, sand, cement, and roofing shingles, among other things.

In another hour these craftsmen all will be at work.

Across town the Morris Maple Paint Store is filled with house painters buying brushes, rollers, buckets, spackling, caulking, thinner, and large amounts of paint.

A coat of paint actually is less than one-twentieth of an inch thick. But it takes a gallon to cover a room of average size and forty gallons—or enough to fill a bathtub—to cover a house of average size inside and out.

At one time paint was available in only a dozen colors. But these days there are over six thousand, from jungle green to lavender blush. Some paints come from the factory ready to use. But most must be mixed in the back room from the directions in a fat book of paint "recipes."

Usually a clerk starts with a can of linseed oil or rubber latex, which is called the "vehicle." Then he adds a white pigment to make sure the color now on the walls doesn't show through. Then he mixes in small amounts of other colors, called "tints," which together produce what the customer has ordered.

The machine on the left measures the pigments and tints in just the right amounts. Then this one, jiggling wildly, mixes them together.

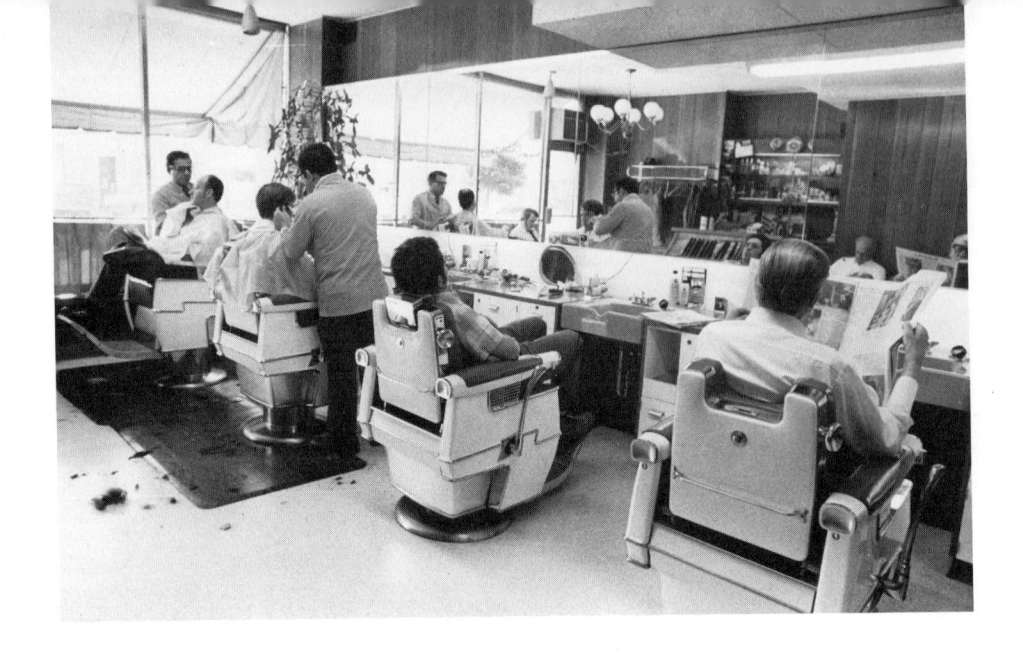

By now most of the barber shops in town have opened. And most are crowded, for many men get their hair cut before they go to work.

A long time ago, barbers also did minor surgery, such as removing a person's tonsils or appendix or sewing up a bad cut. The red and white striped pole outside almost every barber shop is a reminder of that. It stands for a bandage covering a wound.

These days, of course, barbers concentrate on cutting hair. If you aren't getting bald, you probably have over one hundred thousand hairs sprouting from your head, each of which grows a quarter of an inch a month.

The two brothers who run the Continental Barber Shop cut about forty heads of hair a day. Like all barbers, they use scissors, clippers, rubber combs, steam combs, hairbrushes, hair sprays, razors, and lather machines. They also give away about ten pounds of candy a week to customers who don't make a nuisance of themselves.

But every haircut they give is different, because everyone's hair is different and so is the shape of each head. To cut your hair properly (if you're a boy), a barber may make fewer than a thousand snips with his scissors or as many as six thousand. With each snip he may remove as little as a half inch of hair or as much as two inches.

When finally he has shaped your hair so it looks right to him, he tidies up your sideburns . . .

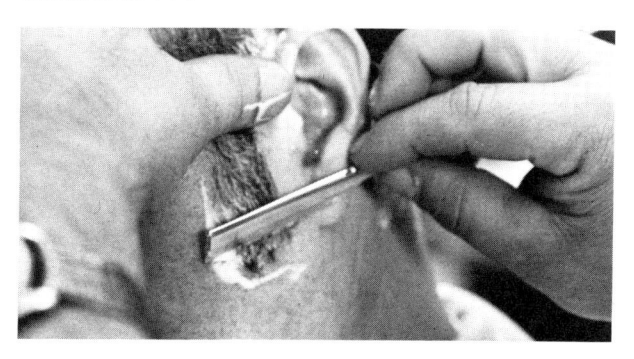

and trims your nose hairs, ear hairs, and eyebrows, and also your beard if you wear one.

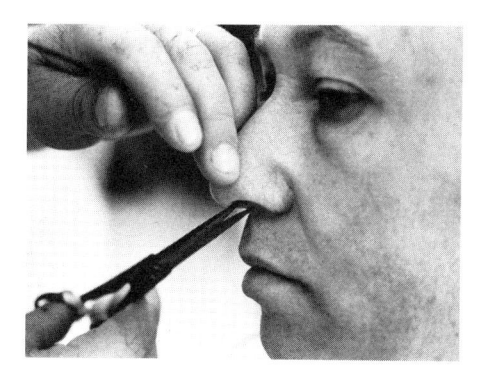

Some barbers start every haircut at the back. Then they move to the left side, then to the right, then to the top. According to superstition, a haircut will not come out right unless they do this. But other barbers pay no attention to such superstitions.

When the barber is finished, he brushes off any loose hairs and holds up a mirror so you can see what he has done.

"You look like a million dollars," he tells you.

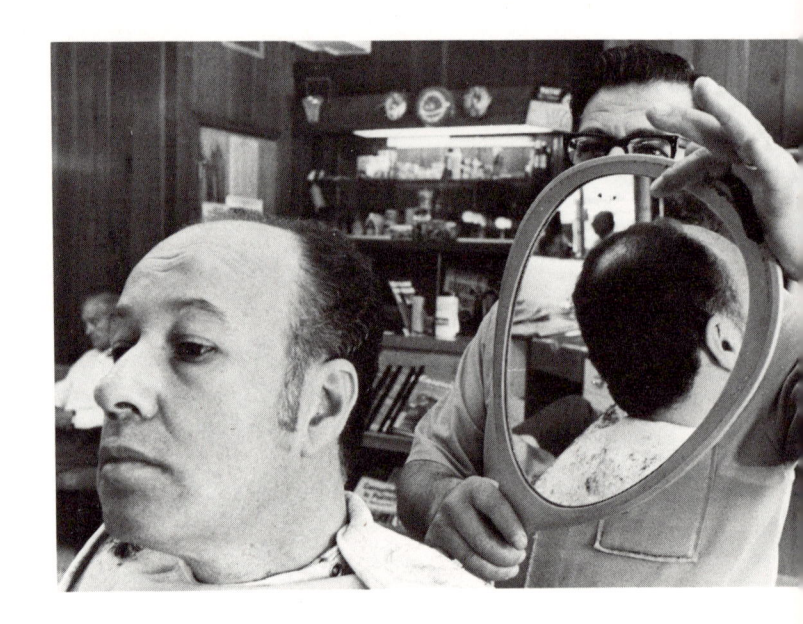

It is about 9:30. By now most of the stores here are open. And the busiest by far are the supermarkets.

On an average day about a thousand customers shop in this Acme market. Together they carry off a half-ton of hamburger, five hundred gallons of milk, a thousand loaves of bread, and over twenty thousand other items, from apples to zippers.

As a result, the biggest job here is keeping enough merchandise on hand. To do so takes constant checking on the store's supplies. But it also takes a warehouse full of groceries, another filled with produce and dairy products, two meat-processing plants, a fleet of trucks, and a computer.

The computer actually is in a building fifty miles away where the company that owns this market, and five hundred others, has its headquarters. Each morning before 10 and each afternoon before 5, the computer rings the manager's telephone to let him know it is ready to take his order.

Using a special code for each product, the manager taps out what he needs on a special machine which is linked to the computer. Each week more than a hundred trucks pull up behind the store with the things he has ordered.

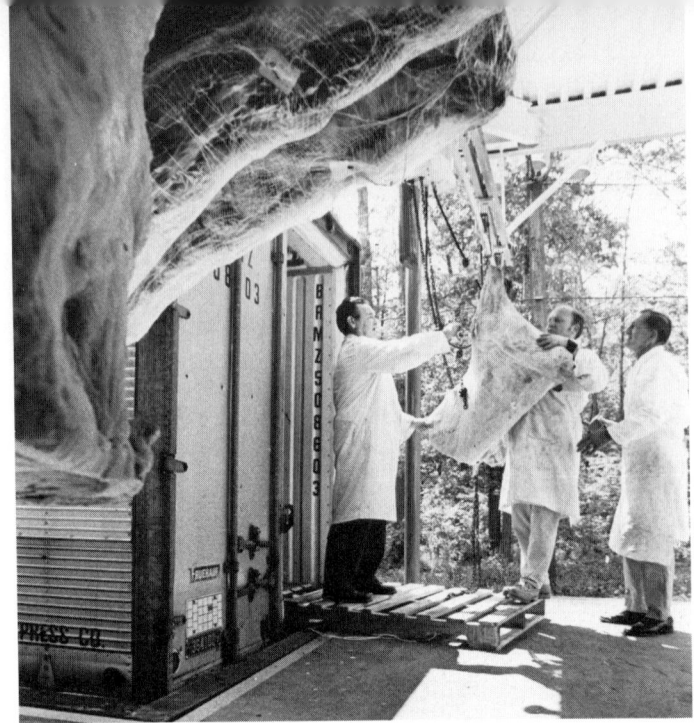

These men are unloading hind quarters of beef and lamb. With band saws and knives, butchers then carve the meat into steaks, roasts, chops, and other cuts and grind what is left into hamburger. To keep the meat from spoiling, they work in 40-degree temperatures, which is about how cold it is inside a refrigerator at home.

As the butchers carve or grind the meat, this woman wraps it in a plastic film and places it on a conveyor belt. When it travels through the "hot box" in front of her, heat seals the plastic wrapping. When the package gets to the other end of the belt, another machine weighs it and automatically figures out what its price should be. Then the machine prints this on a label and sticks the label on the package.

Unloading groceries is far simpler. The only problem is marking each item with the right price, which may change once or twice a week. As we have seen, this is a job that begins each day at midnight.

THE AUTOMATIC CHECKOUT

The next time you buy something in a supermarket, look for a symbol on the package like the one above.

The vertical lines are a special code that tells a computer what the product is and who the manufacturer or supplier is. The numbers are another code for the same information, which can be read without a computer.

These codes are needed to operate the automatic checkout counters a growing number of supermarkets now use. Each has an electronic cash register and an electronic scanner. The scanner is built into the top of the counter near the cash register. It looks like a big square eye. Both the scanner and the cash register are linked to a mini-computer elsewhere in the store.

When a clerk packs your groceries he moves each item, with its symbol facing down, across the top of the scanner.

The scanner reads the vertical lines, then reports what it has read to the computer. The computer makes a record of what has been sold, then reports the current price of the item to the cash register. The item and its price are flashed on a screen facing the customer. And the cash register automatically rings up the sale. All this happens in less than a second.

As the clerk packs the last item, a sales slip listing everything you bought, its price, and the amount you owe the store pops out of the register.

What is the advantage of all this?

For one thing, these machines make it faster for you to check out. They also make it easier for a store to keep track of what it sells and what it must order. They also help the store in another way. They reduce the number of workers it needs, which lowers its costs and raises its profits.

If your basement is full of water and you can't find a plumber, Urken's Hardware will rent you a pump so that you can bail yourself out. Or if your toaster won't toast, somebody there will fix it for you. Or if you need an extra key, he will make you one.

First he places your old key at the front of this machine, where his hand is.

Then he fastens a blank key near the back. It is called a "blank" because it doesn't have notches in it yet.

When he turns on the machine, a metal arm travels slowly up and down the notches of the old key. Meanwhile, a cutting wheel attached to the arm also moves up and down—cutting the same notches in the blank key.

But what is remarkable about Urken's and other hardware stores are the great many things such small places sell. Irv Urken guesses he has at least ten thousand different products for sale. These include "hardware," which means tools and other metal goods, and "housewares," or kitchen equipment.

At Urken's you can buy 34 different kinds of hammers and 21 different kinds of saws and at least 104 different kinds of nails, and also these things:

light bulbs *concrete mix* *pails*
knives *steam irons* *mailboxes*
shelving paper *oil cloth* *ladders*
flashlights *car polish* *hoses*
fertilizer *screwdrivers* *wrecking bars*
seeds *chicken wire* *lubricating oil*
lawn spreaders *garbage cans* *picnic coolers*
wheelbarrows *work gloves* *chisels*
coffee grinders *plumber's pipe* *wrenches*
meat grinders *furnace filters* *shovels*
pots *fuses* *bird feed*
chain *stovepipes* *string*
sockets *bath mats* *baking pans*
drinking glasses *curtain rods* *shades*
clocks *screens* *paint*
clamps *flower seeds* *screws*

And over nine thousand other things.

And the people who work here know where each one is.

The man in the window is mailing pictures of his children to his mother in Greene, Iowa. The Postal Service will ship and deliver them for eighty cents.

After the man gave him the money, the clerk attached eighty cents in stamps to the envelope, then canceled the stamps as proof that the right amount had been paid.

Each year the people here spend over $8 million on postage to mail over forty million postal cards, letters, and packages, which makes the post office one of the biggest businesses in town.

But you also can buy many other products here.

For stamp collectors, the post office sells stamp albums and a history of stamps. It also sells "commemorative" stamps, which mark historical events, and "first day covers." These are beautifully decorated envelopes which are issued in honor of new stamps and postmarked the first day these stamps are available.

The post office also is the only place where you can buy a "bird stamp," which is a license to hunt certain migratory birds, and a full-size copy of the Declaration of Independence.

It also is the only place where you can learn just who the FBI is after these days.

Education Library H-SU RICHARDSON LIBRARY HARDIN-SIMMONS UNIVERSITY ABILENE, TEXAS 79601

25

A bank may not look like a store, but that is exactly what it is. It sells products and services that have to do with money.

One of these services is, of course, protecting money people do not want to keep at home for fear they will lose it or it will be stolen. The banks in this town have over $300 million people have left in their care.

As protection against bank robbery, the First National Bank depends on cameras that photograph anybody who looks suspicious, on automatic timers that permit doors to open only at certain hours, on automatic alarms that bring police on the run, and also on equipment it keeps secret.

It also depends on steel or concrete rooms called vaults. It keeps safes here and also safe-deposit boxes customers can rent to store valuable possessions. This vault is guarded by a solid steel door that weighs five thousand pounds.

To keep a dishonest teller from stealing the money he handles, the bank checks, or audits, each teller without warning several times a year to make sure that his records are correct and that he has the amount of cash he should.

To keep customers from withdrawing more money than they have in their accounts, the bank depends on a computer. When a teller punches a customer's account number on a set of keys, the computer reports just how much the customer has.

One bank in town has an automatic bank teller built into the wall outside its office. The teller's name is Harvey Wallbanker. It helps you to withdraw money from your account even when the bank is closed.

You insert a special plastic card the bank issues, then push the correct numbers—your account number plus four secret numbers. If the computer approves, out comes the cash.

Actually, a bank keeps very little money on hand, only enough to meet its day-to-day needs. The rest is hard at work somewhere else. For when you deposit your money in a bank, the bank may use it to earn money for itself. This is the way it pays its expenses and makes a profit.

Banks use most of their deposits to loan people the money they need to buy a house or a car, or to start a business, or to help pay for a college education, or for other purposes. In return, the people who borrow this money pay the bank interest.

For example, if you borrowed $5,000 to buy a car you might agree to pay it back in three years. Along with the $5,000, you would pay the bank about $1,000 in interest. This is the price it would charge for letting you use its money.

On any given day, the twenty thousand banks in the United States and Canada have over a trillion dollars in deposits out on loan.

Many of their customers have deposited money they plan to save for a long time. But many also deposit money with which they plan to pay bills or to buy something.

Instead of using cash, however, they write checks which then are subtracted from their accounts.

Without this system everyone would have to use cash to pay bills, rent, mortgage payments, salaries, and other costs, which is not practical in a country as big and complicated as ours. Each day, as a result, banks in the United States handle over one hundred million checks.

A PAIR OF SNOWSHOES

A while back I ordered a pair of snowshoes from a store near Brunswick, Maine, where I have a charge account. They cost sixty-five dollars. When they arrived I sent the store a check from my account in Princeton, New Jersey.

I mailed the check on a Monday and it arrived in Maine on Wednesday. The store then deposited my check in its bank. This increased the store's balance by sixty-five dollars.

When the bank in Brunswick examined the checks that came in that day, it sent those from other areas to a clearing house in Boston, which is the nearest big city.

A clearing house is a special bank run by the federal government. Its purpose is to help banks exchange checks without using cash.

My check for sixty-five dollars arrived in Boston on Thursday. The clearing house then did two things. It added sixty-five dollars to the account the Brunswick bank has there, since that money was now part of its deposits. It also sent my check to the clearing house nearest Princeton, which is in Philadelphia.

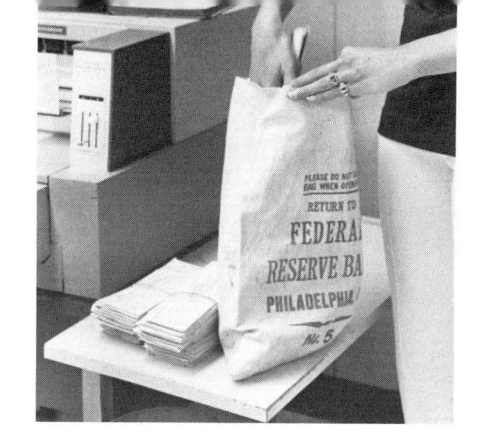

The check arrived in Philadelphia on Friday. The clearing house there then subtracted the sixty-five dollars from my bank's account, since the money no longer was part of its deposits. It then returned the check to my bank.

The check arrived back in Princeton on Monday, a week after I had mailed it to Maine. My bank then subtracted the sixty-five dollars from my account. And that was that.

29

Florence Hillier runs the Flower Basket from a big old-fashioned desk that fills a tiny room at the back of her store. But you are more likely to find her in this big room where she makes flower arrangements. Some are for parties and weddings. Others are to cheer up people who are sick or to honor those who have died.

In every case she starts with a picture in her mind of the kind of arrangement that would be best. Then, with flowers and greenery and wires to hold them in place, she creates what she imagines.

Each morning Mrs. Hillier checks her stock of flowers, greens, plants, bowls, vases, potting soil, fertilizer, and other things. Then she calls her suppliers to let them know what she will need that day.

When the flowers arrive, Mrs. Hillier's helpers immediately plunge the stems into warm water and keep them there for four or five hours. That is how long it takes for the water to rise through the stems to the blossoms.

Then the flowers are placed in a refrigerator until they are needed. This process is called hardening. It keeps flowers fresh long after they are sold.

If you pick your own flowers, you can do the same thing and they will last far longer than usual.

For the potted plants, the problem is different. Mrs. Hillier stocks over a hundred different kinds, and each has different needs for light, water, and warmth. All must be met if the plants are to thrive, and she is to sell them.

Twice a year publishers in this country announce the titles of their new books. Soon after, a steady stream of salesmen come to visit Ralph Shadovitz at the Book Mart on Palmer Square.

Of the forty thousand new titles published each year, Mr. Shadovitz orders about five hundred for his store. Some are best sellers. Others are basic books on sports, crafts, pets, cooking, and other subjects he believes a good bookstore should have. Each year he also orders many books published in previous years.

If nobody buys a book he has ordered, Mr. Shadovitz usually can return it to the publisher within one year without having to pay for it. This is called "buying on consignment." But there are books he keeps anyway because he likes them or because he knows from experience that sooner or later somebody will buy them.

Each day he checks one small section of his bookstore to find out which books are selling, which should be reordered, and which should be returned. It takes him six months to check the entire store. Then he starts all over.

Even so, he cannot tell you just how many books he has. They are all over the place: on shelves that reach to the ceiling, on tables and chairs, even on the floor.

At most stores, nine people in ten who walk in buy something. At bookstores, usually only one in ten does. The reason is that most shoppers have no idea which books they want.

Mr. Shadovitz opened the Book Mart over twenty years ago because he loved books. But running a good bookstore takes sixty hours a week and more, which leaves him very little time for reading—even though there are books all around him.

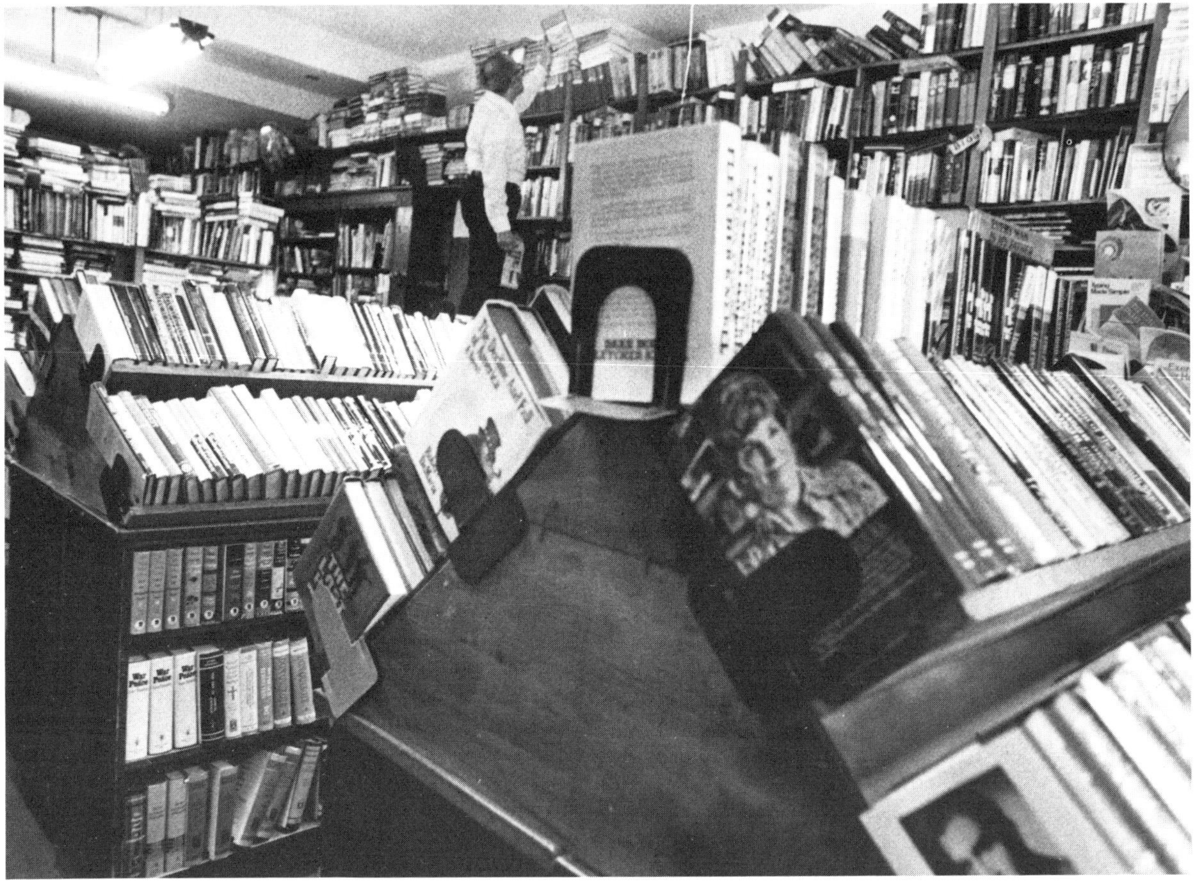

What an art gallery offers for sale depends pretty much on the kind of art the owner likes best and knows the most about. Some art galleries specialize in painting or sculpture or crafts. The Eye for Art, which Helen Benedict owns, specializes in prints.

To make a print an artist first creates an original design. The design is cut in wood, linoleum, or metal, or is drawn on a silkscreen or a slab of limestone. Then the surface is inked and covered with a sheet of paper, under pressure. When the paper is removed, it carries a copy—or a "print"—of the design.

Usually the artist makes from ten to two hundred copies of a design. Each is numbered in the order in which it is printed. If 6/10 is written at the bottom of a print, this means it is the sixth copy out of ten that were made. Each time a print is "pulled," the artist signs his or her name at the bottom as proof that it is an original work.

Some of the prints Mrs. Benedict shows at her gallery are created by artists who live in this area. She gets the rest from "agencies," companies which try to help artists sell their work. If a print is sold, the gallery and the artist share what the customer pays. The artist then pays the agency part of his earnings. Because art galleries are interesting places, often they have many visitors. But since works of art are expensive, not many buy anything. At the Eye for Art about one in a hundred does.

Because of this galleries also may sell art supplies and make picture frames for prints, paintings, needlepoint, photographs, and other things people want to display.

The framemaker here is Jack Koeppel, whose father also was a framemaker. To frame a picture, he first discusses with the customer which of his five hundred moldings—the strips of wood he uses to make a frame—would be best.

Using this chopper, he cuts the four pieces he will need for the top, bottom, and the two sides. He cuts each at a 45-degree angle so that they will fit together perfectly.

He then glues the pieces into a frame, holding them in place under pressure from special clamps. After the frame dries, he strengthens the corners with thin nails and fills the nail holes with wax the color of the wood.

When he finishes he places the picture inside the frame and inserts a stiff backing board behind it to hold it in place. Then he fastens the board to the frame. As the last step, he attaches the picture wire from which it will hang.

A store a university here runs for its students sells over 100,000 phonograph records a year.

The music these records contain comes, of course, from a narrow groove which spirals inward from the rim of the record. What produces the music are about twelve million tiny wiggles in the walls of the groove—deep narrow cuts that create the high notes, wide shallow cuts that create the low notes. As a phonograph needle follows these wiggles, it vibrates. And the sounds the vibrations make come together as music.

The groove actually is so narrow it is almost impossible to see. It is less than two thousandths of an inch across and less than seven thousandths of an inch deep. And it is so tightly coiled, a needle must travel almost a half mile if you play just one side of a twelve-inch record.

To make a record, the music first is recorded on tape. As the tape is played back, a special recording needle cuts a groove in a blank record. As the needle moves around and around, the music from the tape causes it to vibrate. These vibrations cut the wiggles in the walls.

After a record has been "cut," both sides are coated—first with silver, then with nickel—from which metal copies are made. These copies are called "stampers."

They look like records that have been turned inside out, with the grooves coiled on top instead of below the surface.

The two stampers are then locked in a press something like a waffle iron, with one on top and the other underneath. Then soft plastic is poured between them and the press is locked together and heated. When it is opened, a copy of the record is ready—with the grooves and the wiggles just where they belong.

WIGGLES IN RECORD GROOVE

PHONOGRAPH NEEDLE
GROOVE IN RECORD

This may look like a living room. But actually it is part of a large collection of chairs, sofas, tables, chests, mirrors, lamps, beds, and mattresses at a furniture store called Nassau Interiors.

There are over five hundred pieces of furniture crammed into this small store. Nearby a warehouse holds five hundred more.

Along with furniture, you can buy cushions and carpets here and have draperies and slipcovers made and get free advice on which furniture to use and just where in a room to use it.

Leonard LaPlaca selects most of the furniture he sells in his store. He does so each spring and fall at "furniture fairs" in North Carolina where the big furniture companies display their newest products.

But before he orders anything he gives it very careful thought. For if it does not appeal to his customers they will not buy it. And if they do not buy it, it will use space for something they would buy. And if he makes a mistake he cannot return it.

If one of Mr. LaPlaca's choices "moves" too slowly, usually he puts it on sale. If this does not help, he cuts the price again. If it *still* doesn't sell, he may give it away. Or if he likes it enough, he may take it home and use it himself.

You also can buy furniture across the street at Eleanor Waddell's antique shop. An antique is, strictly speaking, a hundred years old or more. As a result, much of the furniture you will find was made before the Civil War and is rare and valuable.

Mrs. Waddell also sells other things people used long ago. The scales in the picture were used by a grocer in the 1830s when Andrew Jackson was President of the United States. And the lamp was used by a university student in the 1770s.

You will also find clocks and crocks, jugs and rugs, paintings and books, and cameras and banjos, which aren't quite so old. There also is a dollhouse a man spent sixty years fixing up. . . .

This is the living room. Altogether there are eight rooms in this house. Each is decorated with miniature furniture its owner made. One room has a tiny organ which plays church music when you crank it. The price of the house is $650, but Mrs. Waddell has not tried very hard to sell it. She likes it too much.

40

Her store also is a good place to buy an old-fashioned top hat, or a swallow-tailed coat (one with two tails), or the "silks" a jockey once used.

Mrs. Waddell buys her merchandise from people who live in town, from other antique dealers, or at auctions. Each Sunday she and her husband also drive their truck into the countryside in search of old things people no longer want and have put away in their attics or barns. Then they try to find a new home for them.

At one time the only shoes people wore were animal skins they wrapped around their feet for warmth and for protection. These days we have more of a choice.

In this storeroom at Hulit's, and in the one behind it, and in the one underneath it, there are over fifteen thousand pairs of shoes. These include everyday shoes, party shoes, overshoes, basketball shoes, track shoes, tennis shoes, hiking boots, riding boots, other boots, sandals, moccasins, loafers, ballet slippers, bedroom slippers, and sneakers, which people buy more of than anything else.

Because children's feet are still growing, children's shoes usually come in ninety-six different sizes, depending on how long and how wide they need to be. But even shoes for adults have as many as seventy different sizes. Each extra size equals about a quarter of an inch. The average shoe size these days for a woman is about a 9 and for a man about a 10.

Actually people today have bigger feet than people once did. Since they eat better and get better medical care, they are stronger and taller and need bigger feet to hold them up—and bigger shoes for their bigger feet.

Charles Tulumalo has a curious problem. Like most people in his trade he is busier than ever. But few people are becoming cobblers these days, and he cannot find the help he needs to get his work done.

As a result, he often stays at his shoe repair shop until 9:30 at night to finish what he has promised his customers for the next day.

This may mean putting new stitches in a pup tent, or changing the color of an old pair of shoes, or adjusting a special shoe that a child with bad feet must wear.

It also means, of course, replacing heels and soles, for after a shoe has traveled five hundred miles or so these parts begin to wear out. It is a job that takes about half an hour.

First, Mr. Tulumalo pries off the old heels, then adds new ones with a machine that makes its own nails from a roll of wire. Next he replaces the soles.

When a shoe is made a manufacturer usually starts with a "welt," a piece of leather you probably have never seen. It looks something like a horseshoe, except that the space inside is filled with cork. The cork behaves like a shock absorber when your shoe strikes the pavement. The "uppers"—what you put your feet in—are stitched to the top of the welt. The sole is glued and stitched to the bottom.

To remove an old sole, Mr. Tulumalo cuts the eighty or ninety stitches that hold it to the welt and pulls it loose. To install a new sole, he first replaces the cork inside the welt.

and stitches it to the welt with a waxed flax thread . . .

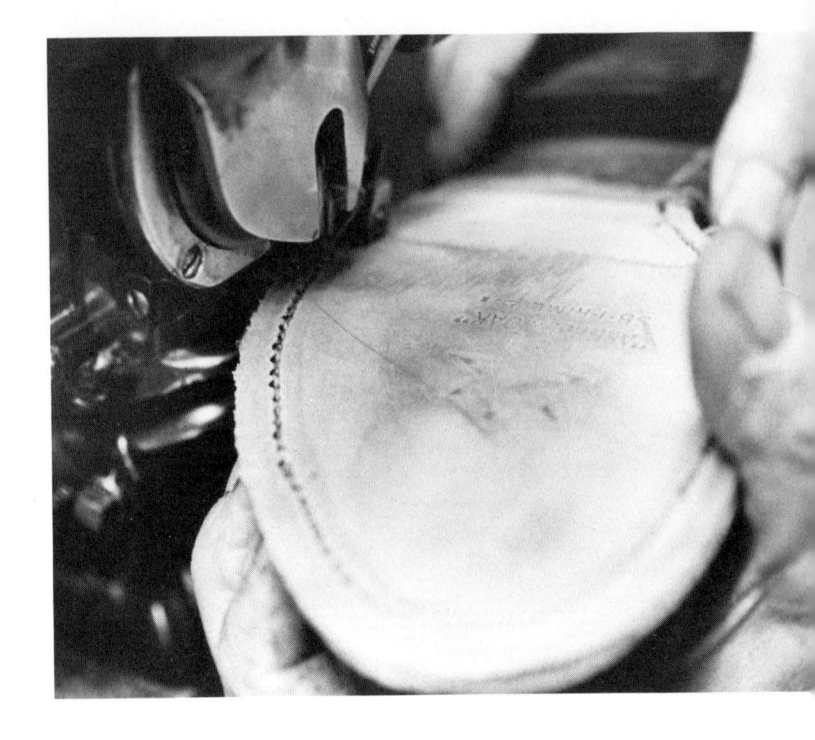

Then he glues a piece of leather to the bottom of the shoe and pounds it in place . . .

and trims it to fit . . .

and trims it again.

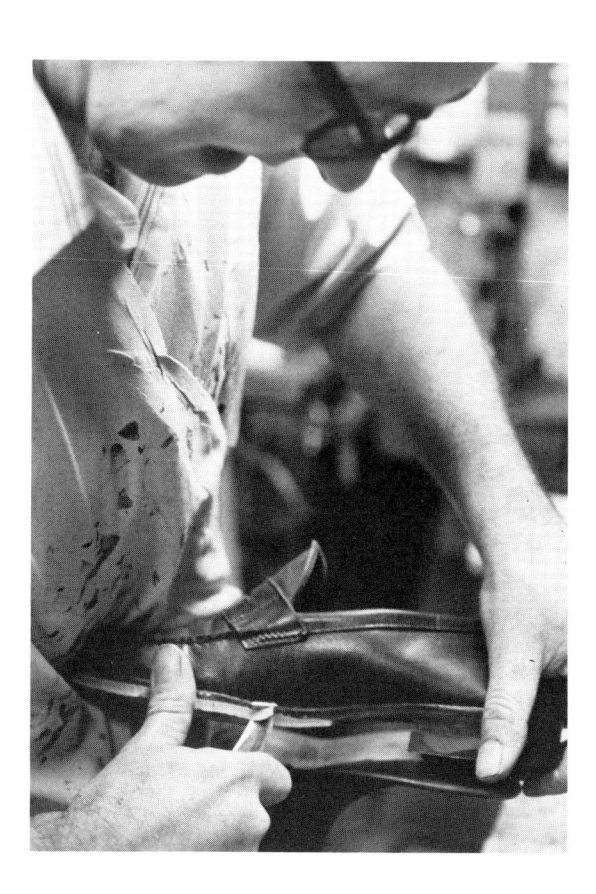

Finally he sands it smooth, colors the edges, and waxes them to keep water out. Then he fixes the other shoe—and moves on to another pair.

If you are a young woman and you want clothes that are lively, yet traditional, one place to try is the Ladybug. If you want clothes that are more offbeat, there is a store around the corner you probably would like better. But both places, like all clothing stores, have the same problems.

One is the need to rebutton, rezip, refold, or rehang all the clothes people look at or try on—and don't buy.

Another is the need to repair clothing customers damage—particularly big, heavy customers who tuck themselves into something that is much too small and pop a button or break a zipper or split a seam.

Another is shoplifting. In an average year, over a hundred young people are arrested for shoplifting and charged with juvenile delinquency in this town. And a hundred others are warned not to try it again.

To protect themselves, some shopkeepers depend on cameras which continuously take pictures of customers or on mirrors which help them to see what is going on when their backs are turned. They also keep a sharp eye on whoever is in their store.

When several persons walk in together, they immediately attract attention, for two or three shoplifters may keep sales clerks busy while another takes what he or she can.

People who wear their coats while shopping also attract attention, as a coat is a good place to hide things. So do people who carry a shopping bag. So do people who look in one direction while their hands move in another.

Selecting the right things to sell is another problem these stores share. What makes the job difficult is that clothing, like furniture, cannot be returned if no one buys it. But this may be less trouble than it seems, for people love clothes.

A typical customer at the Ladybug owns at least a dozen dresses, a dozen blouses and shirts, and a dozen pairs of pants. And there is one who owns 108 pairs of pants.

You can't wash a wool skirt in water. If you do, it probably will shrink.

Instead people take their woolen clothes and other delicate clothes to a dry cleaner's. However, "dry" doesn't actually mean dry. It means that instead of water, the cleaner uses a fluid that dries so fast there is no chance the clothing will shrink.

When you take a pair of pants or a skirt to Louis Verbeyst's shop on Tulane Street, it first is tagged to make sure that everything that is needed is done.

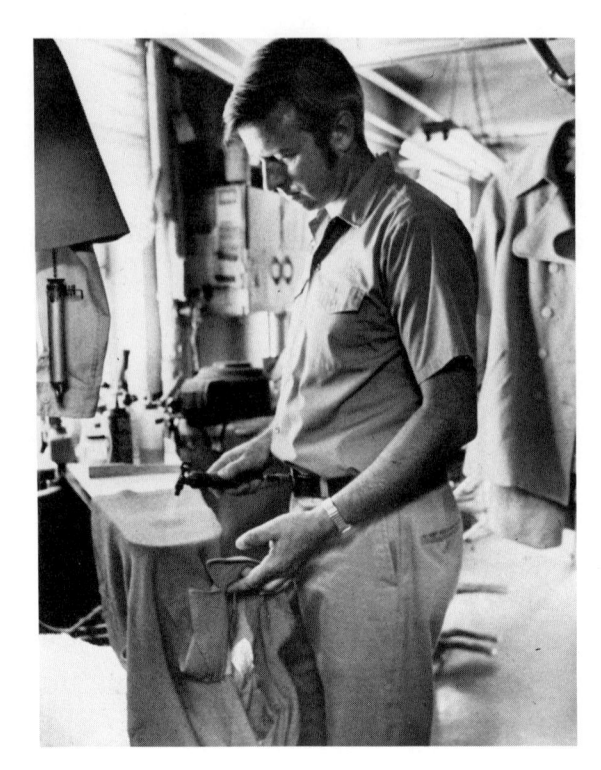

It then goes to this spotter who checks it for stains and uses chemicals, steam, hot air, and a stiff brush to remove those he finds. However, gravy stains are a problem. So are those caused by mayonnaise, ink, and blood.

The clothes then travel upstairs to a "finishing" room...

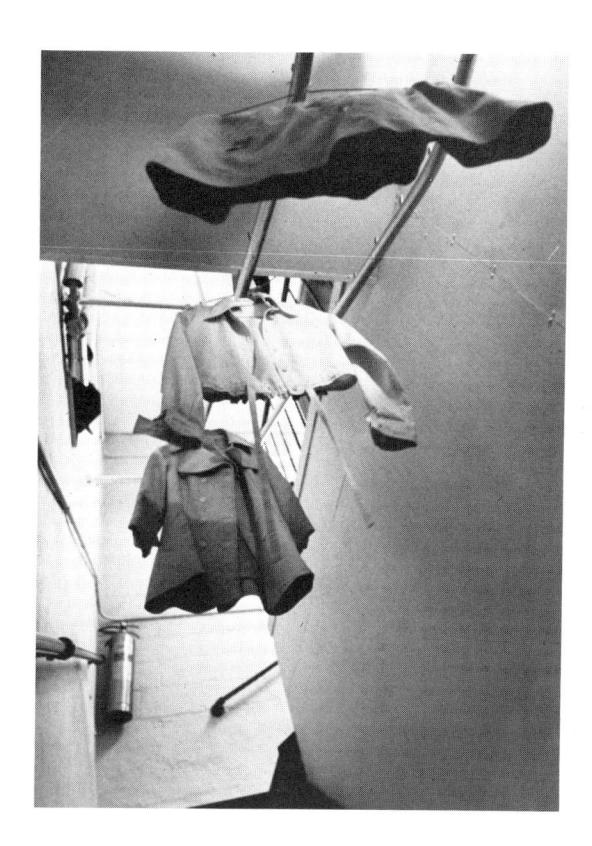

When the spotter has done his best, a batch of clothes is loaded in one of these tanks, washed for a half hour in dry-cleaning fluid, and tumbled dry in a big clothes dryer.

where they are pressed. If a piece of clothing needs special care it is ironed by hand. Otherwise a machine is used. The "iron" in the picture takes wrinkles out of coats and jackets by forcing steam and hot air through them.

Here also leaky raincoats are waterproofed, skirts are re-pleated, missing buttons are replaced, and other repairs are made. Then each order is covered with a plastic bag and hung on a rack until its owner comes to claim it.

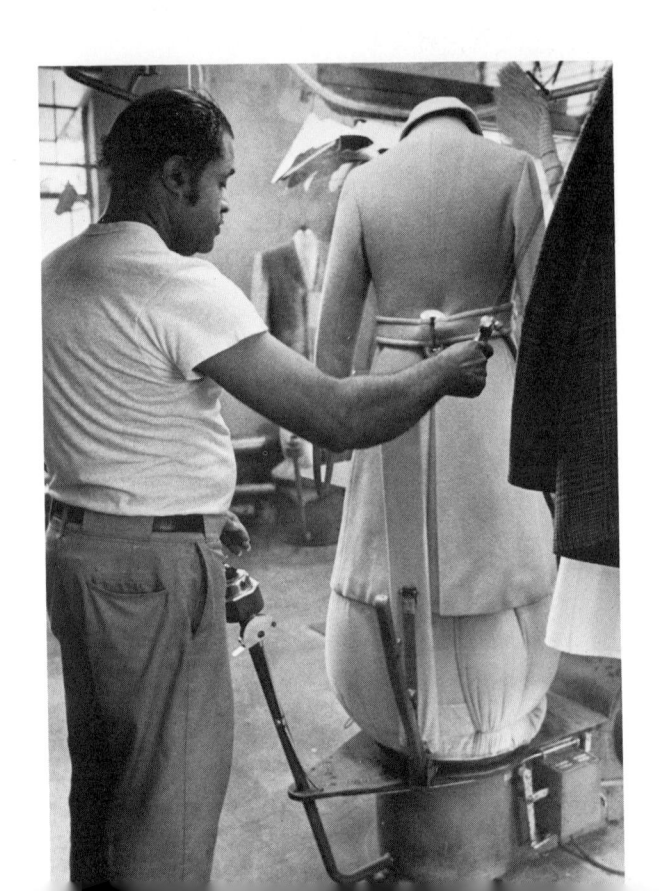

The emerald this jeweler is examining is a rare green mineral called beryl. When a miner dug it out of the ground in Colombia, South America, it weighed about four ounces.

Then a gem cutter carved away the cracks and other defects, cut the sides at angles which caught the light, and polished it until it glowed as if it were alive.

When he finished, the emerald weighed two-and-one-half carats or about one-fiftieth of an ounce. Then a jeweler set it in the ring in the picture which you can buy for $8,500, plus tax.

If a ring with an emerald is not what you have in mind, you might think about one with a ruby or a sapphire or a diamond. Each year LaVake's sells over four hundred diamond rings alone to people who use them as engagement rings or wedding rings.

If you are thinking of getting married, there is a very nice diamond ring here for $6,800. If money is a problem, there are others for as little as $100, but, of course, they are smaller and not so beautiful.

Along with rings, LaVake's sells a great many necklaces, bracelets, and pins. These are made from jewels of various kinds or from gold, silver, or other precious metals. But if you don't see what you want, they will make it for you.

Although jewelry is very expensive, each day sixty or seventy people visit this store. If this seems like a great many, think how beautiful these ornaments are and how much people enjoy them.

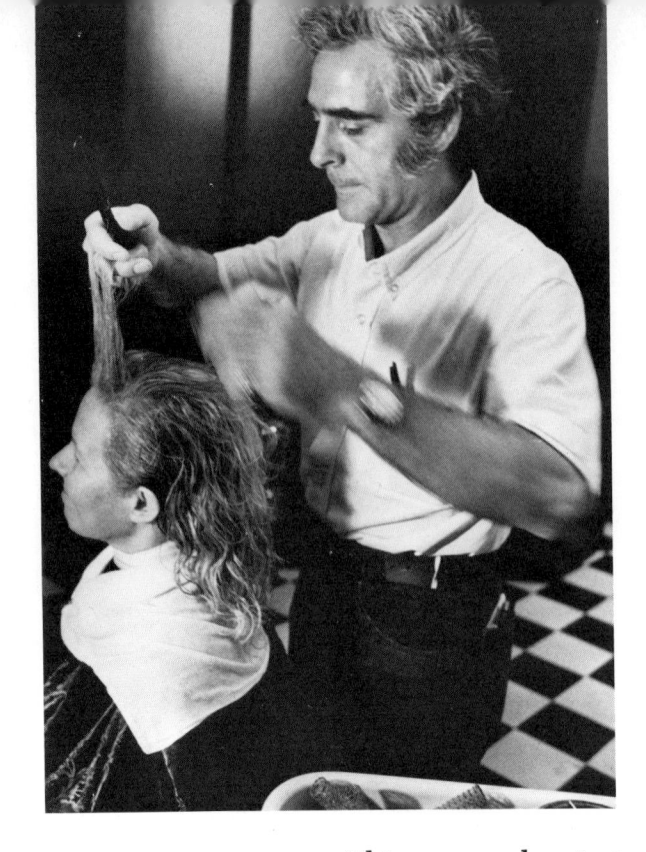

who will have their hair done today at Anthony Scaramozzino's House of Coiffures on Nassau Street. Some of Mr. Scaramozzino's customers come in only now and then. But at least half have regular appointments.

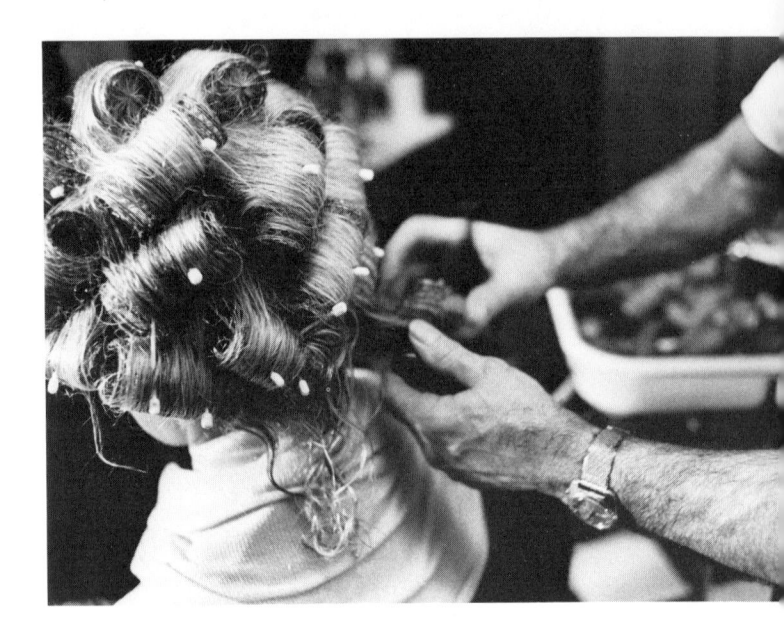

This woman has just had her hair shampooed. Now she is having it set, or arranged, in a particular style. The curlers the hairdresser is installing will keep her hair where he wants it until it dries. Then he will comb it and shape it.

She is one of about twenty-five women

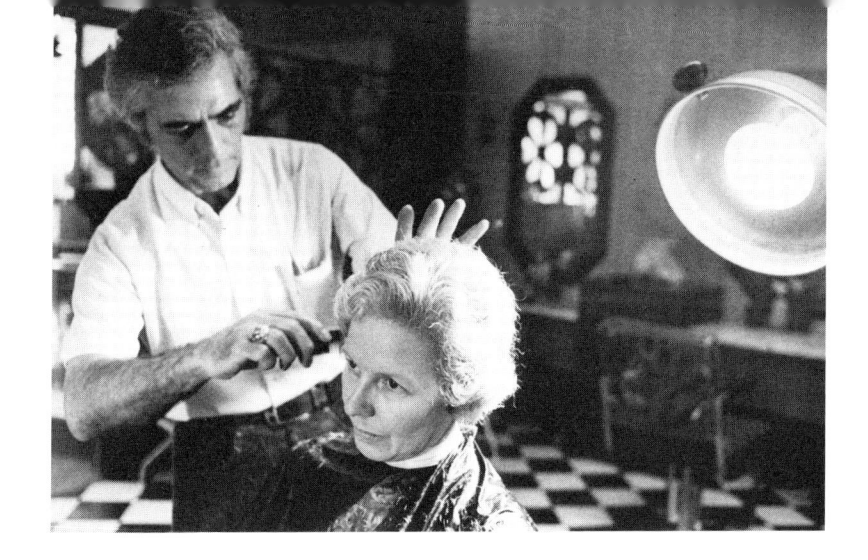

Each week they have their hair washed and set. Each month they have it cut. If they have straight hair and want it curly, every three months they have a permanent wave. This involves the use of chemicals which keep their hair curly for a long time, but not permanently.

To make themselves more attractive, some women also have their hair colored, or their fingernails shaped, or their faces massaged, or their eyebrows plucked.

Usually a customer spends one to three hours at the House of Coiffures each time she has an appointment. If she comes in every week this could cost her $500 a year or more.

But Mr. Scaramozzino cuts his own hair. He takes his scissors in one hand and a small mirror in the other. Then he stands with his back to one of the big mirrors on the wall. This way he can see the back of his head as well as the front.

And he snips away. However, this is *not* recommended unless you are Mr. Scaramozzino or somebody like him.

The woman with the camera is Elaine Miller. With another woman, she owns a photography studio called Pictures. They take pictures of people, pictures of weddings, and pictures for advertising and publicity.

Mrs. Miller took thirty-six pictures of this boy before she was sure that at least some of them would please him and also please her.

The lens of her camera aimed the picture she saw at a strip of photographic film. This film is coated with chemicals which react to light. Each time she clicked her shutter, the film captured the different shades of light and dark that together make up the details of a photograph.

When Mrs. Miller had taken the pictures she needed, she went back to her darkroom. There, in total darkness—just a glimmer of light would have ruined her work—she unrolled the film and placed it in a tank of developing fluid.

The fluid brought out the details the chemicals had captured. In doing so it produced the negatives she needed to print her pictures. With the negatives she made a rough copy, or proof, of each picture she had taken. Then the boy and his parents decided which one they like best.

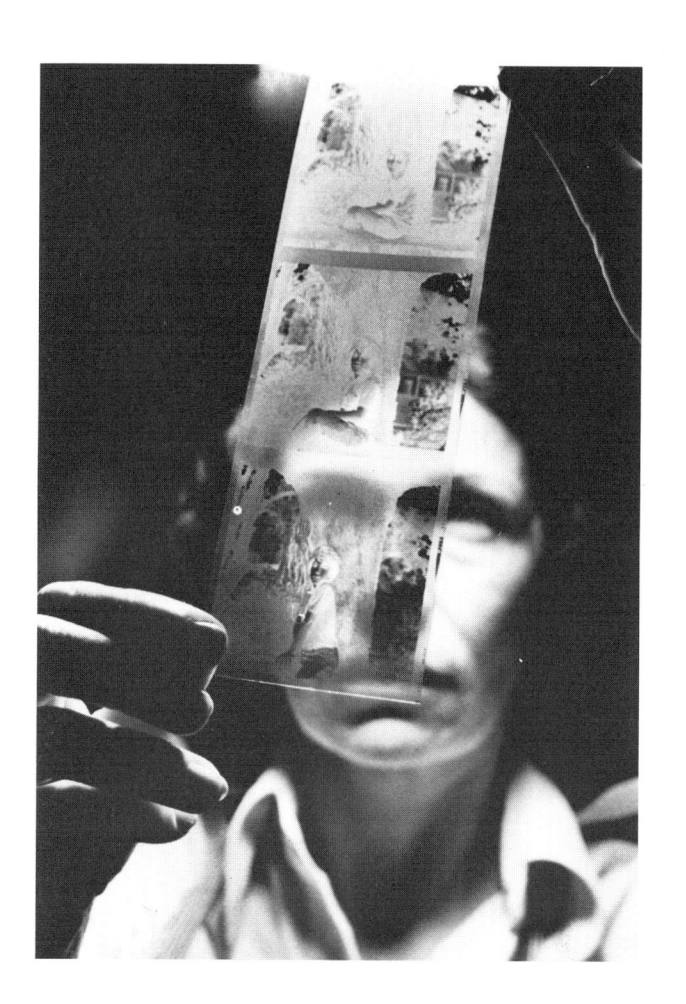

To print this picture in the size they wanted, Mrs. Miller used an enlarger. This machine transfers the picture in the negative to a sheet of printing paper. The paper is coated with chemicals which react to light, like those on the film.

First she inserted the negative in the enlarger, then she placed a piece of printing paper in the bottom. After making various adjustments, she passed a strong beam of light through the negative and the magnifier just below it. The light carried the picture to the printing paper where the chemicals recorded it.

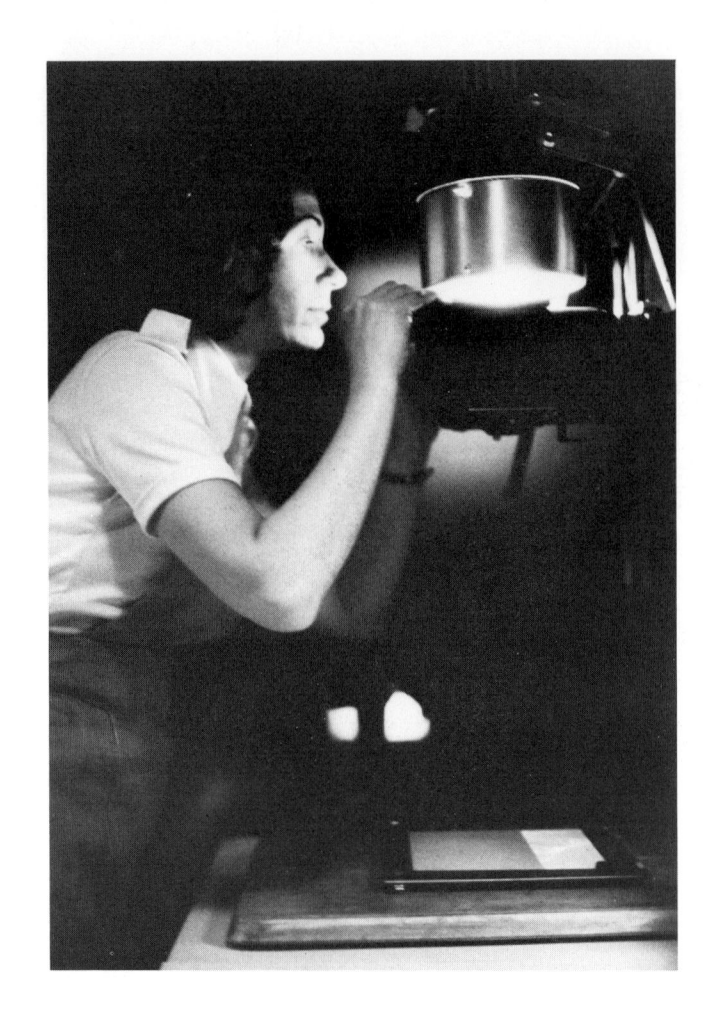

To bring out the picture she soaked the printing paper in a pan of developer. Then she washed the print in a "stop bath" which stopped the action of the developer after it had done its job. Then she washed it in "hypo," a chemical which keeps photographs from fading.

Finally she rinsed it in clear water, dried it, and mounted it on a piece of heavy white cardboard. When she was done, she signed her name in the lower right-hand corner as the photographer whose work this was.

A car is a steel container one-sixteenth of an inch thick. It is made of a dozen or so pieces of metal which are formed by machines into various shapes. These shapes are then fastened together with bolts, rivets, and welding torches. A car also has twenty-five thousand other parts. These enable it to start, move, and stop.

There are in the United States over 110 million cars. Each year 8 million of these end up in junkyards. But each year people buy 10 million more.

At Nassau Conover Motors on State Road you have your choice of thirty different models in thirty different colors. Each has all kinds of optional "extras," from tape decks to power-operated sun roofs. At the other automobile dealers in town, it is pretty much the same.

If you decide you really need a car, remember that it is one of the most expensive things you will ever own. People in the United States spend over $100 billion a year to buy cars and to keep them running. With the average person, this comes to thirteen cents out of every dollar he spends.

For example, you will need to have your car serviced regularly. This means having somebody grease the moving parts and replace dirty motor oil. It also means having your motor adjusted, or tuned, so that it runs the way it should, and replacing your brakes or tires and many of the other twenty-five thousand parts when they wear out.

You will also need to wash your car from time to time, which is good for the car and also makes it look better. If you aren't too busy, you could wash it yourself. But each week hundreds of people here spend at least three dollars to have their cars washed and waxed at F. P. Lawrence's car wash on Alexander Road. They leave their car at one end of this 180-foot tunnel. And they get it back three or four minutes later after it has been hauled through by a conveyor belt.

On its trip it is sprayed with over three hundred gallons of water—first soapy, then clear. At one point it moves through a series of three-foot brushes which automatically scrub the roof, the windows, and the tires.

At another, it passes through these strips of carpet which clean out dents and scratches the brushes can't reach and help remove the wash water.

The car then is sprayed with wax, dried with hot air, and wiped and polished by hand. Meanwhile, the dirty water is cleaned and used again.

Of course, if you aren't careful, or if somebody else isn't, you could dent your fender or bash your bumper or damage your car in some other way. Or damage yourself.

To fix a fender, a body man first removes the seat next to it, then the upholstry next to *it*, then the wheel and tire the fender covers.

With ding hammers, fender slappers, and dolly blocks, he then bangs the fender back into shape, making sure that when he is finished it will look just like the one on the other side.

A painter then paints what has been fixed. With paper and tape, he masks the area he *isn't* going to paint. Next he grinds off all the old paint, sands the fender smooth, and dusts it with an air hose.

When all is ready, he sprays on four separate coats of a special paint which protects the car from rust, then he covers these with six more the color of the car.

The bill? One hundred and thirty-five dollars, plus tax.

Be careful.

When school lets out a surprising number of people head for Kopp's Cycle Shop on John Street to pick up bicycles that have been fixed or to bring in others that need fixing.

Usually the problem is a flat tire or a wheel that bent when a rider jumped a curb. But it could be almost anything since a bicycle may have eleven hundred parts or more.

At one time a bicycle was a much simpler machine. It had neither pedals nor a chain drive nor gears. To make it go, a rider pushed with his feet, then raised them and coasted. It was called a "dandy horse."

But in 1839 a blacksmith in Scotland named Kirkpatrick Macmillan added something like pedals to his dandy horse and something like a chain drive, and bicycles began to change.

If you are thinking of buying a new bicycle and need advice, Mr. Kopp will fill your ear. For example:

- Save enough money to buy a good bicycle.
- Make sure it is guaranteed for at least a year.
- Have it adjusted after one month, then after six months, then every twelve months.
- Oil it regularly. But find out what to oil, how much oil to use, and how often to do so.
- Keep it out of the rain.
- Don't jump curbs.

If you do these things, Mr. Kopp says your bicycle will last for years and years.

Back in the Middle Ages, candy was used mostly by doctors to disguise the taste of the medicines they prescribed. Usually this candy was made from white sugar, rose water, something called gum dragon—and medicine.

At the candy store Polly Lyons runs on Palmer Square, people buy over three tons of candy a year, none of which will cure a disease.

If you have a pocketful of money, consider the mints (there are fifty-two kinds), or a pecan fritter, or a chunk of white chocolate two inches thick, or a French truffle, made of many layers of chocolate, each a different color.

If you don't have a lot of money, try a peppermint stick or a licorice whip or a package of red-hot dollars or jackstraws or violet crumbs.

No matter what you buy, it is likely to contain a sugar syrup with various flavorings. If it is chewy, like fudge, it probably was cooked at 225 degrees, or what is called the "soft ball" temperature. If it is hard, like a root-beer barrel, it probably was cooked at about 300 degrees, the "hard crack" temperature.

With a store full of candy, one of Mrs. Lyons' problems is the amount of moisture in the air. If there is too much, her candy loses its flavor. As a result, she is the only storekeeper in town who protects her merchandise with a humidifier. This is a machine that keeps the amount of moisture at a particular level.

In running a candy store, she also has another problem—self-control. For each time she eats her candy, she eats into her profits.

When a waitress pulls the lever toward her, two ounces of cola syrup leave one tank and ten ounces of carbonated water leave the other and mix on their way to the glass. Each day at Buxton's ice cream shop over two hundred people order one of these drinks.

However, even more people order ice cream. The average person in this country eats almost a gallon of ice cream a month. This makes ice cream our most popular dessert. But nobody knows who invented this dish. All we know is that it probably appeared first in the 1500s or 1600s in Italy, and that its ancestor was water ice, what today we call "sherbet."

The ice cream we eat is a mixture of cream (or milk) and sugar, eggs, and flavorings. It also contains cornstarch or gelatin. This keeps ice crystals from forming when it is made or when it is stored. It also keeps the ice cream from melting too fast after it is served.

Under this spigot where no one can see them are two five-gallon tanks side by side. In one is a cola syrup brewed from the nuts of the kola tree and other ingredients. In the other is carbonated water, or soda water.

These ingredients are cooked and cooled, then whipped smooth, and frozen. When you take a bite, the temperature of the ice cream is about ten degrees above zero. But the air beaten into it when it is whipped makes it seem warmer.

About half the ice cream people eat is vanilla. About a quarter is chocolate or strawberry. The rest includes over four hundred flavors, from peanut butter to prune.

A lot of this ice cream is, of course, sold in ice-cream cones or sundaes. It is said that the ice-cream cone first was used at a world's fair in St. Louis in 1904. The sundae is supposed to have appeared just a few years later.

As the story goes, some towns in the Middle West outlawed the sale of both liquor and soda pop on Sundays because of religious beliefs. To keep his customers, a man who ran a soda fountain concocted a dish he called a "Sunday Special." We call it a sundae.

Buxton's big achievement is the Big Bux. It fills a half-gallon container, but it is not hard to make. It is just hard to eat it all.

The Big Bux

You will need the following ingredients:
- *2 bananas*
- *2 scoops each of vanilla, chocolate, strawberry, and butter pecan ice cream*
- *1½ ounces each of crushed cherries, crushed pineapple, strawberries in strawberry syrup, and chocolate syrup*
- *1 pint of whipped cream*

Cut one banana from end to end in quarters. Arrange the pieces close together at the bottom of the container. Place one scoop of each of the four flavors of ice cream on top of the banana.

Cut the second banana as you did the first. Arrange the pieces on top of the ice cream. Place one scoop of each of the four flavors on top of the second banana.

Pour the syrups and the fruit over the ice cream. Cover the whole thing with whipped cream in the shape of a pyramid one foot high.

This boy's hobby is collecting miniature trains. The ones he collects are built to the HO gauge, which is half the size of the O gauge. This means they are exactly eighty-seven times smaller than the engines and cars from which they are copied.

If you are interested in such trains, they also are built to the OOO gauge, the OO gauge, the N gauge, the TT gauge, and the Z gauge—all of which are even smaller.

This boy is looking over the trains at Hoge Woolwine's hobby shop on Nassau Street. The diesel engine he is examining is an exact copy of a real engine fifty feet long.

Since Mr. Woolwine opened his shop almost fifteen years ago, he has learned enough to have a hundred hobbies, including wood carving, working in leather and clay, building model ships and rockets, collecting model trains, and flying model planes by radio.

As a result, he not only sells supplies, he also helps customers build models, plan track layouts, use telescopes, and do countless other things. He also makes repairs and, in emergencies, he makes house calls. In fact, late one Christmas Eve when the author of this book could not put together a set of trains he had bought for his children, Mr. Woolwine showed him how.

"ROBYN" TO "HOBYN" TO "HOBBY"

In England five hundred years ago people called a horse "Robyn" or "Roby" and a small horse "Hobyn" or "Hoby." From "Hoby" it was but a step to "hobby horse," a toy horse young children like to ride for fun. And from there it was another step to "hobby," a different activity with which people have fun.

If you yearn for a snake, the easiest place to find one is at a pet shop called Noah's Ark.

This snake is a garter snake that lived at the Ark until a short time ago. Then somebody bought it and took it home in a plastic bag. At that point the snake was a year old and a foot long. If the person who bought it takes good care of it, the snake should live another nine years and grow another three feet.

A snake is not exactly the kind of pet everybody wants. Yet each week four or five people buy one. Each week a dozen guinea pigs also leave the Ark for other homes. So do a dozen hamsters and gerbils, two dozen mice, two hundred tropical fish, and a parakeet or two.

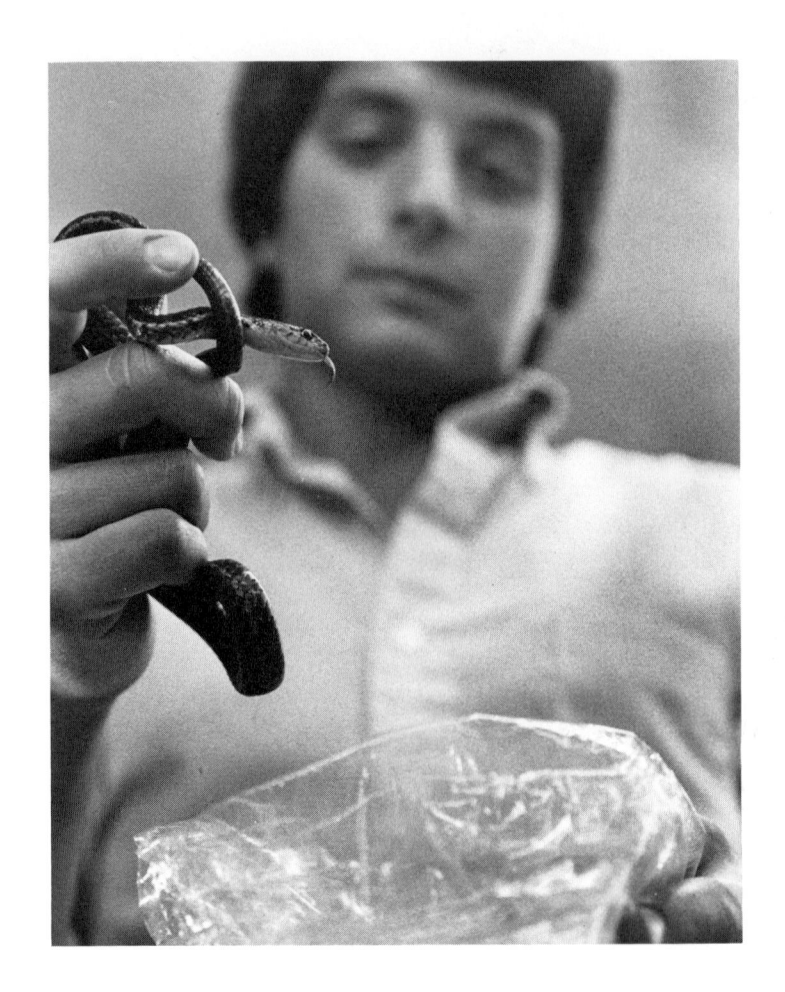

The Ark buys its guinea pigs, hamsters, gerbils, and mice from boys and girls who live in this town. These boys and girls buy a male and a female, raise the litters their animals produce, then sell them.

The snakes, birds, and fish come from suppliers in many parts of the world who collect them or breed them, or both.

Nine families in ten have at least one pet of some kind.

As a result, each week about a thousand customers come to the Ark for dog leashes, rabbit leashes, carrot-juice sticks, bird food, feeding bowls, hamster litter, aquarium plants, and other things, including more pets.

If you would like a puppy, one place to try is J. P. O'Neill's kennels a mile or two south of town.

Mr. O'Neill buys his puppies from several hundred farmers in this area who raise dogs as well as crops. Whenever one of them has a litter ready, he sends Mr. O'Neill a postal card.

Each Tuesday at dawn Mr. O'Neill stuffs the latest cards into one of his pockets, loads his big open truck with turkey crates, and drives into the countryside.

When he returns the next morning he may have with him as many as a hundred pure-bred dogs, all about seven or eight weeks old.

After they are unloaded, he gives each an injection and a dose of medicine. The injection protects them against distemper, a serious disease for dogs. The medicine destroys any worms they may have in their bodies. Then each puppy is placed in a large pen with others of the same breed.

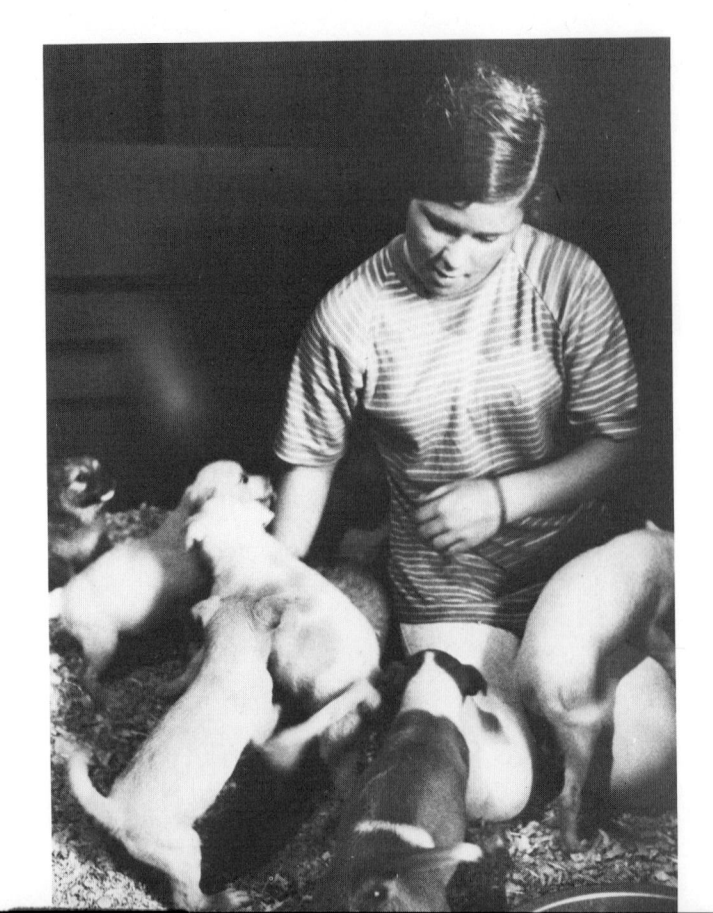

There are over two hundred breeds of dogs. Of these, Mr. O'Neill usually has forty or fifty in stock. To be sure he has the kinds his customers want, often he will lend a farmer a male and a female for breeding.

The dog was the first wild animal man trained to live with him. But that was thousands of years ago, and then there was only one breed. It looked like a wolf, which was its ancestor.

If you decide to buy a puppy, Mr. O'Neill has this advice: Make sure you can return the dog if it is not healthy; have it examined by a veterinarian as soon as possible; give it all the love you can.

When this eye doctor examined this girl, he found she was nearsighted. This means she can see things clearly when they are close to her, but not when they are at a distance. It is the most common problem people have with their eyes.

So that she could see properly, he prescribed eyeglasses with a particular kind of lens. To get the prescription filled, the girl's mother took her to Charles Mraz, one of the opticians in town.

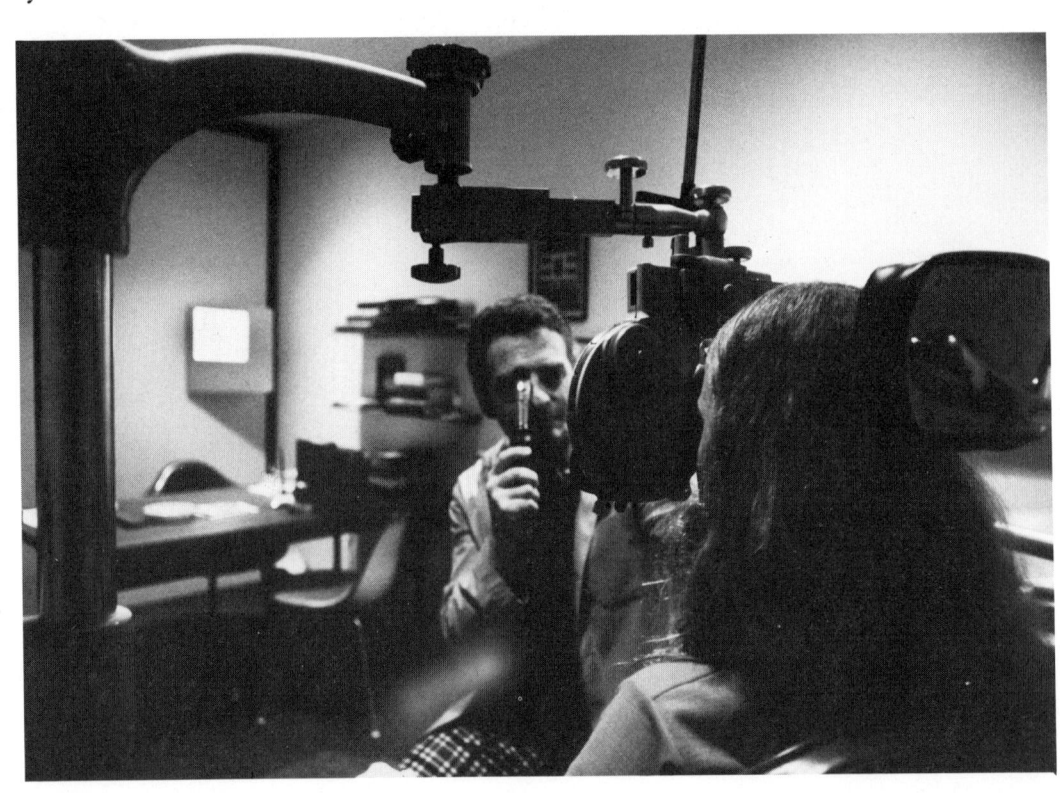

Mr. Mraz first measured the distance between the center of her left eye and the center of her right eye, which told him the size frame she needed. Then she chose the style she wanted. But this was not easy since there were hundreds to choose from, and each one she tried made her look different. When she made up her mind, Mr. Mraz told her to come back in a week.

Through careful measurements he then located the "optical center" of each lens. If a prescription is to work, this must be directly in front of the center of the eye.

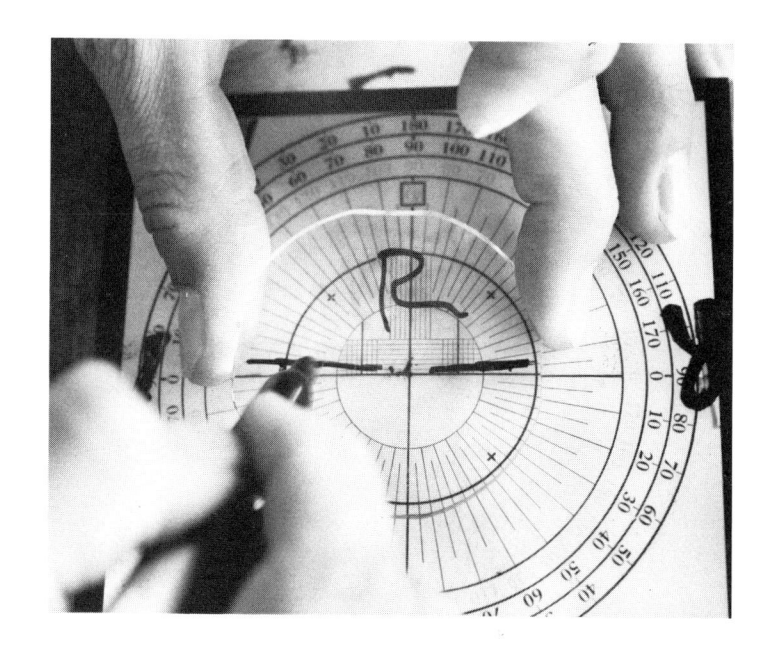

With a grinding wheel he then shaped the lenses so that they would fit the frame. Using the marks he had made as a guide, he set the wheel so that the optical center would be in the right place. Then he attached a pattern the same shape as the openings in the frame, and flipped a switch —and the wheel did the rest.

After the lenses had been shaped, he heated them in an oven for five minutes at 1180 degrees. This toughened them so that they would resist breaking.

To make sure they were strong enough, he placed one lens at the bottom of this plastic cylinder and dropped a steel ball on it from a height of four feet. Then he tested the other lens.

When they did not chip or crack, he installed them in the frame.

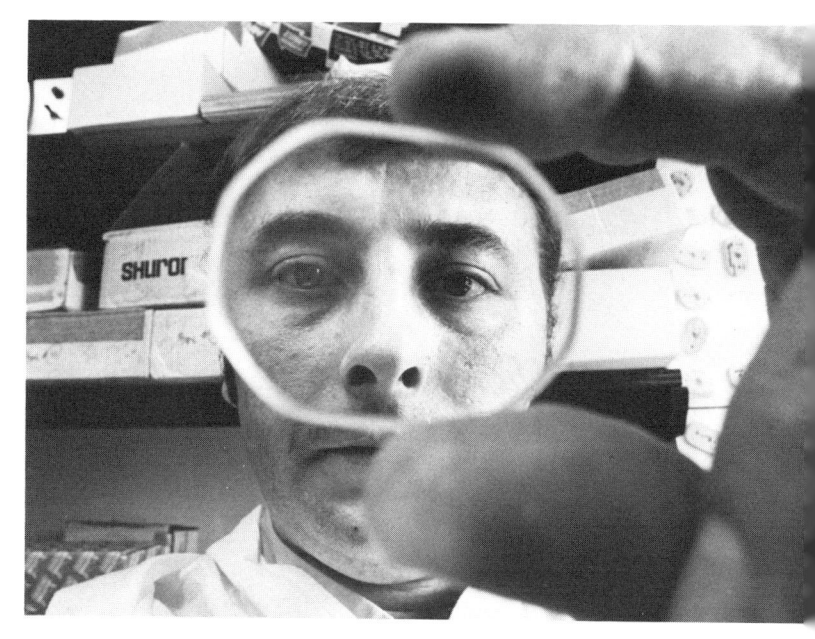

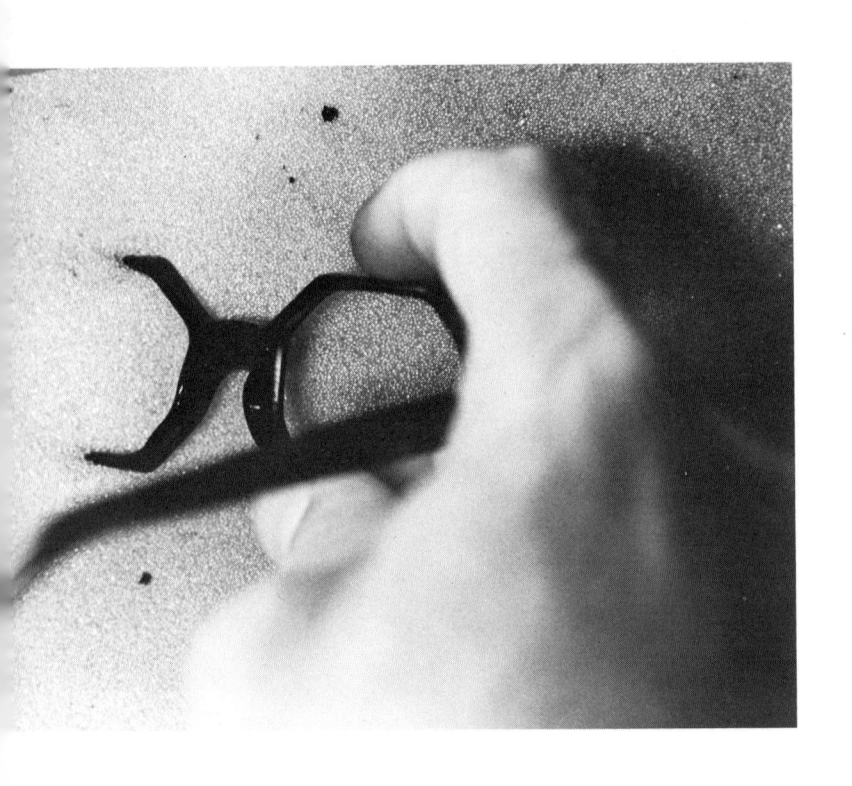

Since the girl selected a plastic frame, he dipped it in a container of hot glass beads which softened the rim. He then pushed the lenses into place. If the frame had been metal, he would have fastened the lenses in with tiny screws.

20/20 VISION

About half of us have eyes which do not work the way they should. If your vision is 20/20, that means you can see from 20 feet what you should be able to see from 20 feet. That is, you probably have normal vision.

If your vision is 20/40, you have to be 20 feet away, or less, to see what someone with normal eyes can see from 40 feet. And *that* means you should visit an eye doctor.

When the girl came back for her glasses, she carefully examined herself in a mirror. Then she took a new look at the world.

It is 4 P.M. and the First National Bank has been closed for about an hour. But the people over at its computer center are still hard at work. Their job is to figure out how much money each of the bank's customers has left in his checking account.

To do this they must know how much money people added to their accounts today and how much they withdrew through checks they wrote.

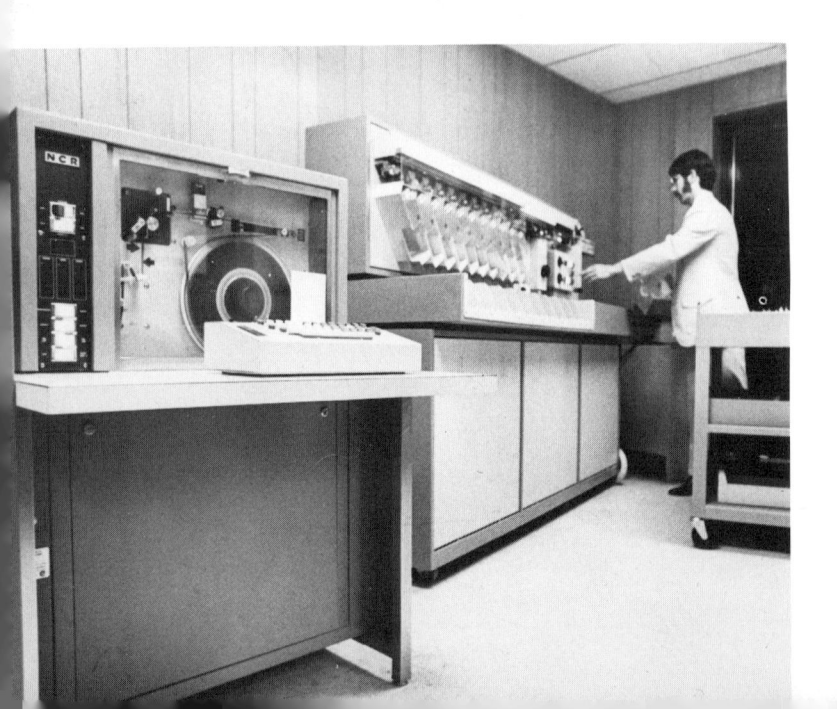

As deposit slips come in, clerks type on each in a special code the amount the customer deposited. The code looks like this:

⑈30⑈44 28⑈7⑈   ⑈000000 27 15⑈

The figures at the left are the customer's account number. The ones at the right are his deposit. The clerks also must "encode" in this way checks customers have written which have been cashed and returned to the bank.

The computer then "reads" each of the deposit slips and each of the checks. As it does, it records the account numbers and the amounts of money involved on a reel of tape. By the end of the day it has filled ten thousand feet of tape with this information.

During the night another computer adds the deposits, subtracts the checks, and prepares a new tape which shows how much each customer now has.

Meanwhile, a worker makes miniature photographs of each check so that the bank will have a permanent record of them in case an error is made.

The checks themselves are returned to the customers once a month. They also get a statement which lists all the deposits they have made and all the checks they have written.

It is after 6 P.M. By now most of the stores here have closed. And most storekeepers have taken to their banks the money they took in during the day. If the bank was closed, they unlocked a small door in one of its walls. Then they dropped their deposit down a chute into a vault called a night depository. However, several also left a few bills and coins in their stores in some secret place, so that they will have the change they need when their first customers come in tomorrow.

One of the few stores still open is Marsh's, a drugstore on Nassau Street.

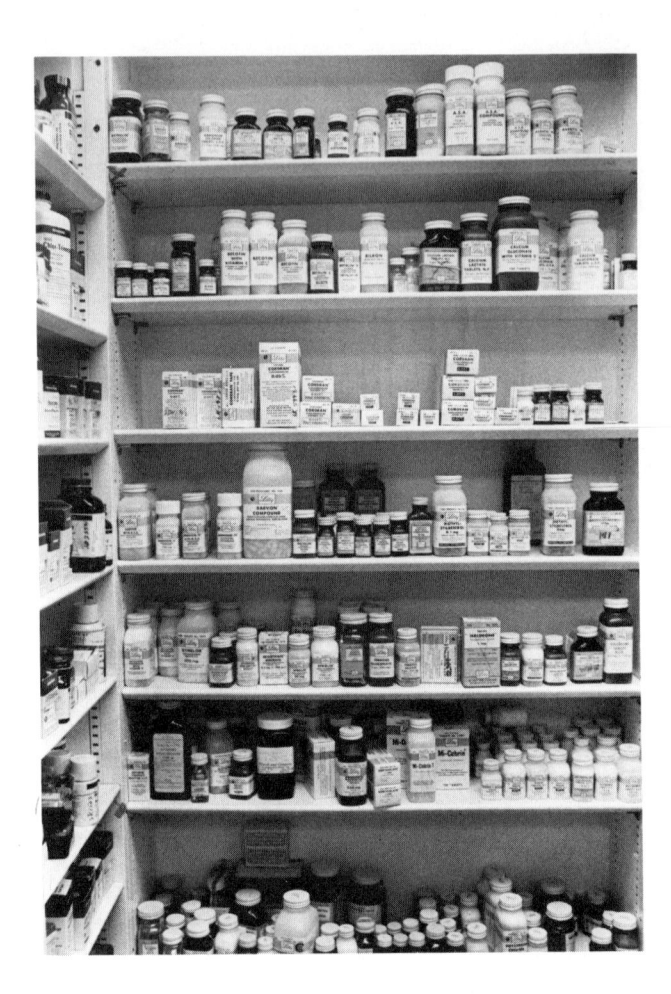

When the first drugstore opened in Baghdad fifteen hundred years ago, the pharmacist prepared all his own medicines. Today, pharmacists buy what they need from big drug companies. This pharmacist at Marsh's has on his shelves more than four thousand different medicines. And what he does not have he quickly can get.

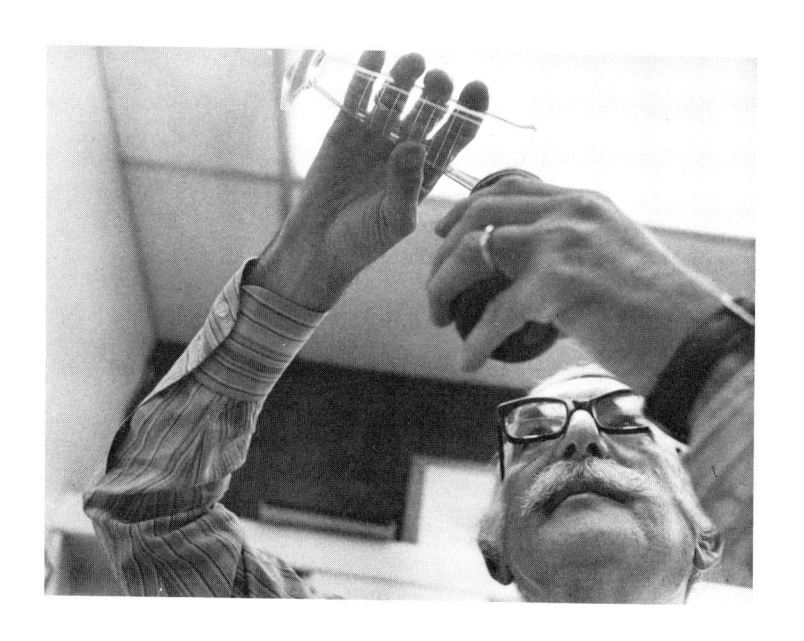

But to find him you first must find your way through a maze of razor blades, shaving creams, beauty creams, false eyelashes, hair curlers, hair coloring, hair tonics, deodorants, and other things.

Each day the three pharmacists at Marsh's fill over one hundred prescriptions that doctors and dentists send in. Most are used for one of four purposes: to fight infection, to kill pain, to help somebody relax or sleep, or to remove excess fluid that collects in the legs or other parts of the body, a problem older people sometimes have.

When a pharmacist fills a prescription he enters it on a card he is supposed to keep for every customer. The card lists each medicine purchased, the amount, when it was "dispensed," who prescribed it, any medicines that disagree with the customer, and any serious medical problems he has. If a customer becomes sick and his doctor isn't available, or if a customer changes doctors, this could be useful information.

As protection against mistakes in prescribing medicines or in filling prescriptions, each prescription a pharmacist handles must be kept for five years.

The next time your doctor writes a prescription for you, get him to explain just how the medicine will work and how it will help. Also ask him to explain the meaning of the Latin abbreviations he uses in his prescriptions.

For example, "q3h" stands for *quaque 3 hora,* which means "every three hours"; "tid" stands for "three times a day"; "qid" means "four times a day"; and "PRN" mean "as needed."

You also may find on your prescription the letters "Rx." These mean "Use the following ingredients." But they also stand for the ancient Greek god Rex who, doctors once believed, could help a medicine work.

At about 9 P.M. the pharmacist at Marsh's locks up. So do the other pharmacists in town. Until tomorrow the only one on duty will be in the pharmacy at the hospital. If you need a prescription filled, he will take care of it.

Bamberger's department store also is open tonight. As a result, the only escalators in town are hard at work. While one moves customers from the first floor to the second, the other moves them from the second floor to the first. Each escalator travels about ten miles a day.

But most of the people who come to this store do not come to ride the escalators. They come to buy clothing, shoes, wigs, cosmetics, shampoo, sheets and pillowcases, pots and pans, drinking glasses, silverware, toasters, suitcases, writing paper, toys, and other things.

A thousand customers or more may visit this store each day. With so many products and so many customers, Bamberger's is one of the most complicated stores around.

It has twenty-four departments, each with its own manager.

It has fifty sales clerks and a half-dozen cashiers to ring up sales.

It has a team of stock clerks who unload merchandise, attach price tags to each item, and bring sales clerks what they need.

It has "shoppers" who check competing stores to learn what they are selling and what their prices are.

It has "buyers" who select the merchandise the store has for sale. Each is an expert in a particular field, such as children's clothing or cosmetics. In making decisions on what to buy, they rely on their experience, on what the managers, sales clerks, and "shoppers" tell them, and on what tickets like these report.

When a customer purchases something, one of these tickets is torn from the price tag and dropped in a box. The holes identify the product, the season of the year for which it was purchased, the department where it was sold, and the manufacturer. The ticket in the picture came from a size 11 blouse in a print design which the store purchased for the spring season.

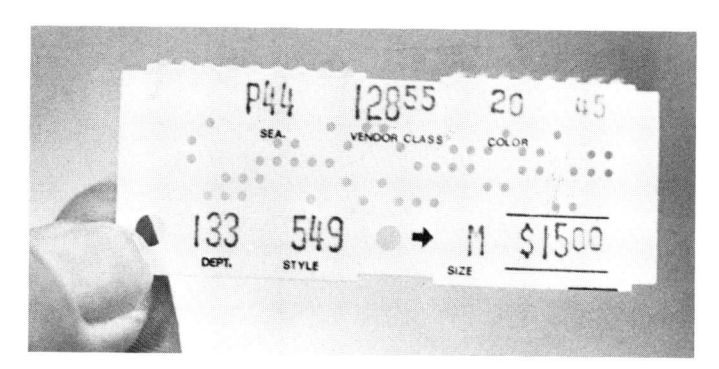

When a customer bought the blouse, the cash register which rang up the sale punched holes in a paper tape which identified the product and its price. Once each week a computer reviews the sales tickets and the paper tapes and reports on how well each product is selling.

The store also has workers who help customers with questions or complaints they have.

It also has a decorator who decorates each of the departments and the display windows.

It also has office workers, telephone operators, repairmen, and janitors.

And it also has people who hire the other people who work here and who teach many of them their jobs.

By 9:45, however, everybody has gone home.

At the Grotto restaurant, sixty-five people—all the restaurant will hold—are eating dinner. In the kitchen, the cook and his helpers rush about filling orders for spaghetti, lasagna, manicotti, gnocchi, and other dishes they started earlier in the day. Meanwhile, another twenty people wait for seats.

By the time the restaurant closes at midnight, the waitresses will have served over three hundred meals. And the busboys will have cleared each of the twenty tables five times. And the dishwasher will have washed fifteen hundred dishes, seven hundred glasses, and fifteen hundred knives, forks, and spoons, and put them all away.

Then, the people who work here have a glass of wine and talk for a while, and go home—until tomorrow.

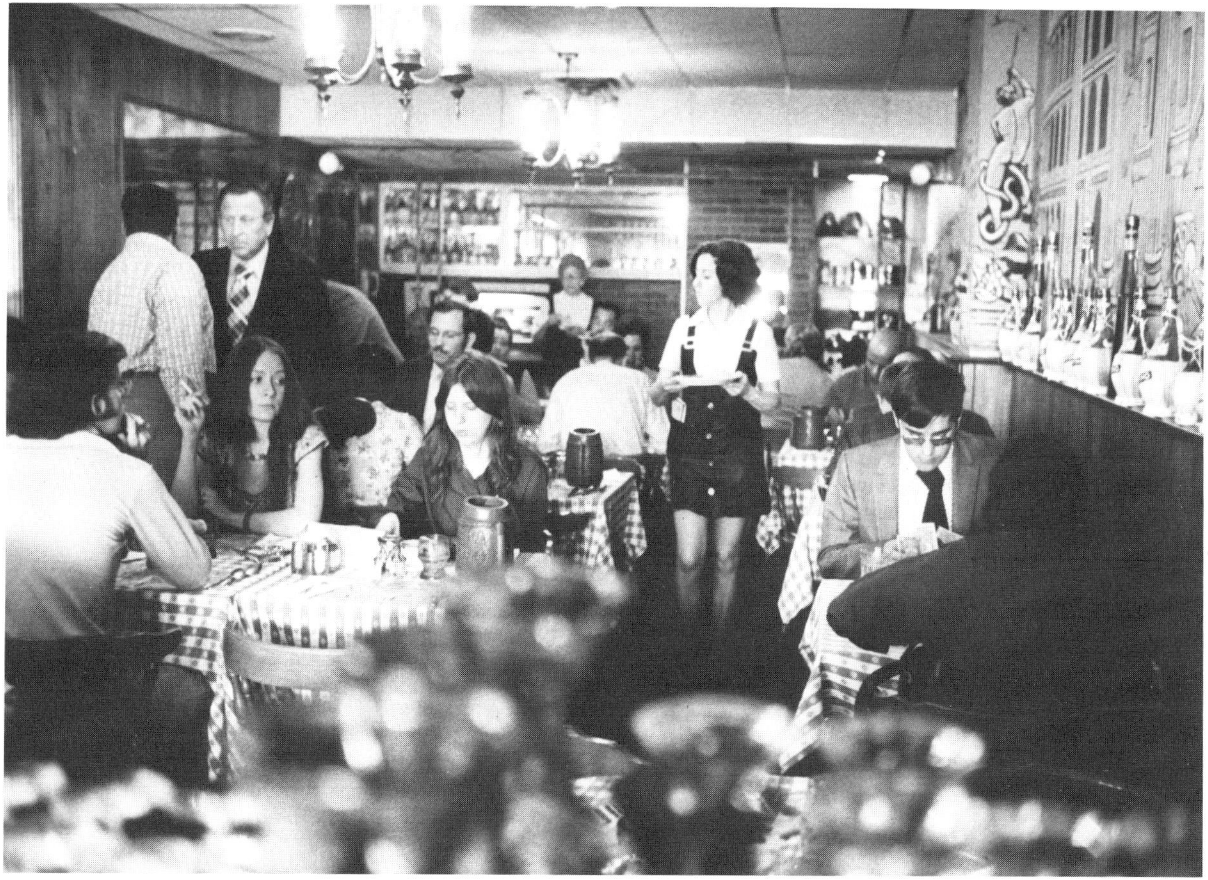

At the Playhouse about eight hundred people are watching this movie. But they do not see what they think they do.

Instead of a "moving picture," what they actually are watching is a continuous series of still photographs, or "frames," each of which shows a slightly different part of the action. But they are flashed on the screen so rapidly, no one would know he was watching one photograph after another. Each second, in fact, he sees twenty-five of these photographs.

In this theater the movie is thrown on the screen by two projectors from a tiny booth 150 feet away. Each projector holds a reel of film that plays for twenty minutes.

Three seconds before a reel runs out, an oval, a dot, or some other symbol appears in the upper right-hand corner of the screen. This warns the operator to get ready to shift to the other projector.

When the symbol appears again, the operator pushes a button and the second projector takes over. Then he reloads the first projector and waits for the next signal.

The screen at the Playhouse is a plastic-coated sheet of canvas forty feet wide and sixteen feet high. To make a film seem more lifelike, the screen curves slightly away from the audience.

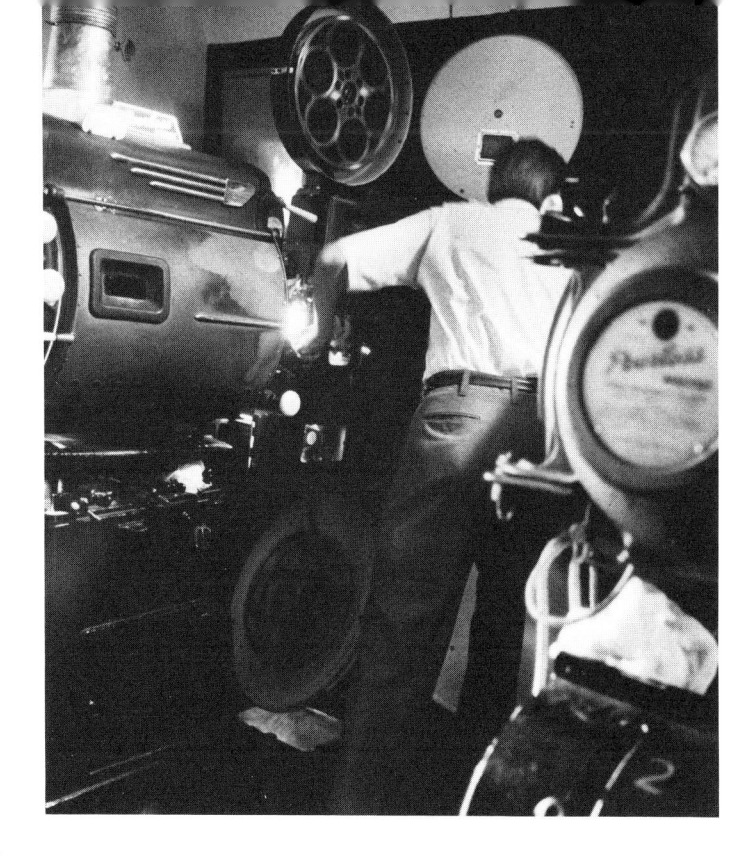

To make the sound seem more lifelike, there are three speakers at different points behind the screen. When an actor speaks, his voice comes from the speaker closest to him. Then it passes through thousands of tiny holes in the canvas.

The owners of a movie theater usually do not decide on their own which films they will show. Usually they make this decision with a "booker" whose business it is to supply films to many theaters. Frequently he also decides how long a film will run.

To show an average movie, the owners of a theater may pay a booker half the admission fees they receive during the first week, then less for each additional week. For the most popular films, they may pay him 90 percent of what they take in the first week, then less for each of the following weeks.

After the movie is over, be sure you don't leave anything behind. When the lights come on ushers at the Playhouse find all sorts of things: umbrellas, eyeglasses, books, coins, handbags, wallets, groceries, even homework. Not too long ago, one usher found a set of false teeth. But so far nobody has claimed them.

Actually, bowling is a very old game. Ancient Egyptians bowled thousands of years ago. So did ancient Germans, but they used war clubs as pins and round stones as balls. The ancestor of the game we play is called ninepins, a Dutch game that used nine pins instead of ten.

What you are looking at is the back of a pinsetter. David Burrough has twelve of these contraptions at his bowling alley, six upstairs and six downstairs.

Although it is almost midnight, they still are hard at work removing tenpins, replacing them, and returning bowling balls to bowlers.

Each of these machines has two sets of pins. While one set is in use, the other is in back waiting for the bowler to finish his turn.

Although bowling has changed in many ways over the years, one thing that has not changed is the skill you need to win. For the most part, this depends on how carefully you roll the ball, not on how fast you do it.

If you are right-handed, try to place the ball between the "1" and the "3" pins in the chart. If you are left-handed, try for the space between the "1" and the "2" pins.

Also, get somebody to teach you how to hook a ball as you release it. After it knocks down the first two pins, the ball will turn slightly, then head up the middle—and the pins will fly and your score will climb.

It is 2 A.M. The bowlers have finally gone home. But at the Uptown U-Wash people still are doing their laundry.

Unlike other stores in town, this one never closes. At almost any hour you probably will find somebody here washing shirts, socks, and underwear. During the day the customers usually are mothers or fathers with their children. But at 2 A.M. they are people who work late, or enjoy staying up, or can't get to sleep.

Like most laundromats, this one has no sales clerks—only machines. For the right amount of money a washing machine will wash sixteen pounds of dirty clothes in thirty-five minutes. For more money, another machine will dry them in about forty minutes. Still other machines will sell you soap, bleach, laundry bags, candy bars, and soft drinks, and will make change if you need any.

These machines also protect themselves against thieves. If somebody tries to steal their coins, they sound an alarm at police headquarters which quickly brings a patrolman.

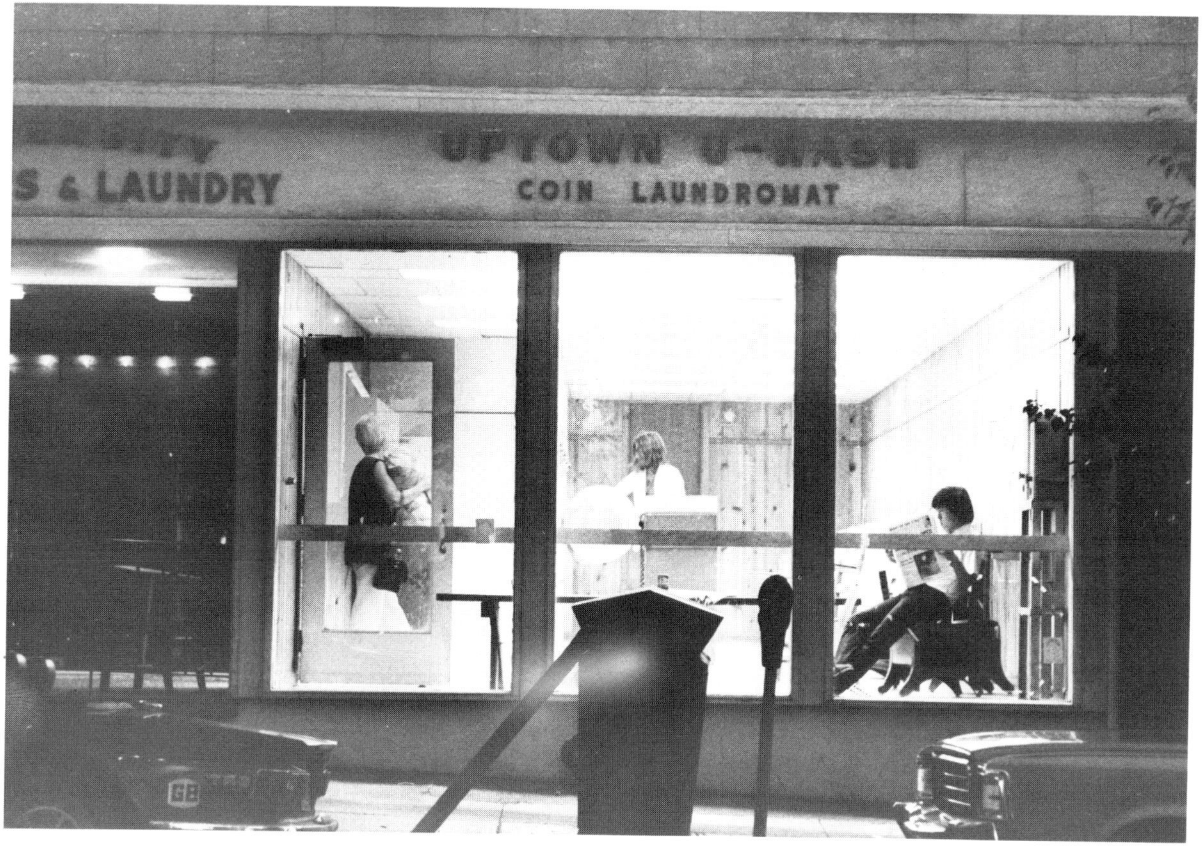
S & LAUNDRY
COIN LAUNDROMAT

Meanwhile, at the Acme supermarket, four men are unpacking groceries, fruit, and vegetables.

In another hour, Alfred Goetz and John King will begin making bread, cakes, and pastries.

At 6 A.M. Mike Pilenza will start his spaghetti sauce.

At about the same time a machine at the First National Bank automatically will type a report which lists how much money each of the bank's customers has in his or her checking account.

By 7:30 Will's service station will be open. Soon after so will the Continental Barber Shop and Urken's Hardware and most of the other stores in town. For the storekeepers here another day will begin.

THE STORES IN THIS BOOK

Acme supermarket, 4, 19–22, 100
Balt Bakery, 1, 4–5, 11, 100
Bamberger's Department Store, 90–92
Book Mart, 32
David Burrough's bowling alleys, 96–97
Buxton's Ice Cream Shop, 69–71
Continental Barber Shop, 16–18, 100
Eye for Art gallery, 34–35
First National Bank, 11, 26–28, 84–85, 100
Flower Basket, 30–31
Grotto Restaurant, 6–8, 92
Grover Lumber Company, 13
House of Coiffures, 54–55
Hulit's Shoes, 42–43
Kopp's Cycle Shop, 66–67
Ladybug Clothing Store, 48–49
LaVake Jewelers, 53
F. P. Lawrence's car wash, 62–63
Polly Lyons' candy store, 68

Marsh's Pharmacy, 86–89
Morris Maple Paint Store, 14–15
Charles Mraz, opticians, 78–82
Nassau-Conover Motors, 60
Nassau Interiors, 38
Noah's Ark pet shop, 74–75
J. P. O'Neill's kennels, 76–77
Phonograph record department,
    University Store, 36
Pictures photography studio, 56–59
Playhouse movie theater, 94–95
Charles Tulumalo's shoe repair shop, 44–47
United States Post Office, 25
Uptown U-Wash laundromat, 98
Urken's Hardware, 3, 23–24, 100
Verbyst's dry cleaners, 50–52
Eleanor Waddell's antique shop, 39–41
Will's service station, 11–12, 100
Hoge Woolwine's hobby shop, 72–73

ACKNOWLEDGMENTS

I am grateful to the following persons for their help in creating this book:

ACME SUPERMARKET—*G. L. Beiswinger, Anthony J. Camillo, Jack Ennis, Barry Hoffman, Peg Localio, Danny McDonald, Alan Schlegel, Tom McNally, Fred Verdi, Charles R. Weber.* ANTHONY'S HOUSE OF COIFFURES—*Anthony Scaramozzino, Eileen Zulla.* BALT BAKERY—*Alfred Goetz, Mrs. Alfred Goetz, John King.*

BAMBERGER'S DEPARTMENT STORE—*Suzanne Guelin Weiss.* BUXTON'S ICE CREAM SHOP—*Robert Buxton, Lester G. Wolfgang, Jr., Margaret L. Wolfgang.* CONTINENTAL BARBER SHOP—*Anthony Sferra.* COUNTRY ANTIQUES—*Eleanor Waddell.* EYE FOR ART ART GALLERY—*Helen J. Benedict, Graeme Keller, Jack Koeppel.*

FIRST NATIONAL BANK—*Wesley G. Cawley, Harrison Cottingham, G. C. Dollar, Arthur L. Everett, Nicholas J. Panicaro, Vera M. Rose, Elizabeth H. Smith.* FLOWER BASKET—*Florence Hillier, Anne Marie Palaro.* GROTTO RESTAURANT INC.—*Betty R. Pilenza, Mike Pilenza, Selia Skillman, John M. Smith, Umberto Tedeschi, Clarence W. Wiley.*

GROVER LUMBER COMPANY—*Royal Craig, Craig Dalton, William J. P. Geddes, Peter Lynch, Jimmie Miles.* HULIT'S SHOES—*Charles J. Corrigan, Ralph T. Hulit, Sr., Warren M. Hulit.* KOPP'S CYCLE SHOP—*Frederick Kuhn, Norman Mastrup.* LADYBUG CLOTHING STORE—*Barbara Barker, Stanley Cohn, Janet H. Lindsley, Penryn Tracy.*

LAVAKE JEWELERS—*Samuel M. Kind, Edith M. Minnick, Eda M. Nicholson, Philip P. Porado.* MARSH AND COMPANY PHARMACY—*Alan Lopez, Benjamin B. Peltin.* MORRIS MAPLE & SON PAINT STORE—*J. V. Skillman, Mike Skillman.* NASSAU HOBBY & CRAFTS—*Charles Sculerati, Hoge Woolwine.* NASSAU INTERIORS—*Leonard La Placa, Cay C. Norman, Vincent Sassman.*

NASSAU CONOVER MOTOR COMPANY—*Ruth Ann Conover, Thomas E. Freer, Edward Gallagher, Alex Kalapis, Frank Kovacs, Art Lombardo, David Long, Albert Mattera, Ronald Naylor, Samuel Price.* NASSAU SHOE REPAIR—*Charles Tulumalo.* NOAH'S ARK PET SHOP—*Richard C. Eldred, Drew Foster.* O'NEILL'S KENNELS—*J. P. O'Neill.* POLLY'S FINE CANDY—*Polly J. Lyons.*

PRINCETON BOOK MART—*Ralph Shadovitz.* PRINCETON CAR WASH—*William Buckalew, Larry Carpenter, F. P. Lawrence, Robert McKinley, Joseph E. Samuels.* PRINCETON PLAYHOUSE MOVIE THEATER—*Richard W. Knight, Ralph B. Quick.* PRINCETON RECREATIONAL CENTER BOWLING ALLEYS—*Chuck Burrough, David H. Burrough.*

PICTURES PHOTOGRAPHY STUDIO—*Pryde Brown, Elaine Miller.* PHONOGRAPH RECORD DEPARTMENT, PRINCETON UNIVERSITY STORE—*Frank Durkin, John Morreals.* UPTOWN U-WASH LAUNDROMAT—*M. F. Vernoia.* UNITED STATES POST OFFICE—*Basil Ferrara, Edward Dlablik, Jr., Michael Ouskin.* URKEN SUPPLY COMPANY—*Deborah L. Huntington, Dave Slater, William R. Sponholtz, Sr., Eunice Urken, Irv Urken.*

VERBEYST DRY CLEANERS—*Bertha Jacobs, Lucille Leath, Robert Owen, James Reed, Charles M. Thaxton, Louis Verbeyst.* WILL'S SERVICE CENTER—*Stephen B. Dean, Vilis Muiznieks.*

Charles D. Allen, Maureen Cosgrove, Betty Ruth Curtiss, Christopher Lamb, Charles J. Mraz, Richard Niehanic, Gerald A. Patterson, Judith S. Shaw, Bailey W. Symington, Bart Smith, Richard B. Walker, and Barbara, Nancy, Elizabeth, John, and Peter Schwartz.

A. S.

INDEX

alarms, in banks, 26
antiques, 39–41
art gallery, 34–35
auctions, antique, 41
automatic bank teller, 28
automatic checkout, 2, 22
automobiles, *see* cars

bakery, 4–5, 100
bank loans, 28
banks, 2, 11, 26–29, 84–85, 86, 100; *see also* money
barber pole, 16
barber shop, 16–18, 100
beauty salon, 54–55
bicycle shop, 66–67
bicycles, 66–67
bird hunting, license for, 25
books, 32
bowling, 96–97
butchers, 20–21

cameras, 56; in bank, 26; in clothing store, 49
candy, 68
car: dealer, 60; repairing, 64–65; wash, 62–63
cars, 60–65

cash registers: department store, 91–92; supermarket, 22
checkout, automatic, 2, 22
checks and checking accounts, 11, 28, 29, 84–85, 100
clearing houses for banks, 29
clothes, 48, 49; dry cleaning, 50–52; washing, 98
clothing store, 48–49
codes, product, 20, 22
computers: in banks, 2, 11, 84–85; in department stores, 92; in supermarkets, 2, 19–20, 22
consignment, buying on, 32

Declaration of Independence, 25
department store, 90–92
dogs, 76–77
doll house, 39–40
drugstore, 86–89
dry cleaning store, 50–52

escalators, 90
eye doctor, 78, 83
eyeglasses, 78–82

FBI wanted lists, 25
Federal Reserve Bank, 29

104

PRINCETON BOOK MART—*Ralph Shadovitz*. PRINCETON CAR WASH—*William Buckalew, Larry Carpenter, F. P. Lawrence, Robert McKinley, Joseph E. Samuels*. PRINCETON PLAYHOUSE MOVIE THEATER—*Richard W. Knight, Ralph B. Quick*. PRINCETON RECREATIONAL CENTER BOWLING ALLEYS—*Chuck Burrough, David H. Burrough*.

PICTURES PHOTOGRAPHY STUDIO—*Pryde Brown, Elaine Miller*. PHONOGRAPH RECORD DEPARTMENT, PRINCETON UNIVERSITY STORE—*Frank Durkin, John Morreals*. UPTOWN U-WASH LAUNDROMAT—*M. F. Vernoia*. UNITED STATES POST OFFICE—*Basil Ferrara, Edward Dlablik, Jr., Michael Ouskin*. URKEN SUPPLY COMPANY—*Deborah L. Huntington, Dave Slater, William R. Sponholtz, Sr., Eunice Urken, Irv Urken*.

VERBEYST DRY CLEANERS—*Bertha Jacobs, Lucille Leath, Robert Owen, James Reed, Charles M. Thaxton, Louis Verbeyst*. WILL'S SERVICE CENTER—*Stephen B. Dean, Vilis Muiznieks*.

Charles D. Allen, Maureen Cosgrove, Betty Ruth Curtiss, Christopher Lamb, Charles J. Mraz, Richard Niehanic, Gerald A. Patterson, Judith S. Shaw, Bailey W. Symington, Bart Smith, Richard B. Walker, and Barbara, Nancy, Elizabeth, John, and Peter Schwartz.

A. S.

INDEX

alarms, in banks, 26
antiques, 39–41
art gallery, 34–35
auctions, antique, 41
automatic bank teller, 28
automatic checkout, 2, 22
automobiles, *see* cars

bakery, 4–5, 100
bank loans, 28
banks, 2, 11, 26–29, 84–85, 86, 100; *see also* money
barber pole, 16
barber shop, 16–18, 100
beauty salon, 54–55
bicycle shop, 66–67
bicycles, 66–67
bird hunting, license for, 25
books, 32
bowling, 96–97
butchers, 20–21

cameras, 56; in bank, 26; in clothing store, 49
candy, 68
car: dealer, 60; repairing, 64–65; wash, 62–63
cars, 60–65

cash registers: department store, 91–92; supermarket, 22
checkout, automatic, 2, 22
checks and checking accounts, 11, 28, 29, 84–85, 100
clearing houses for banks, 29
clothes, 48, 49; dry cleaning, 50–52; washing, 98
clothing store, 48–49
codes, product, 20, 22
computers: in banks, 2, 11, 84–85; in department stores, 92; in supermarkets, 2, 19–20, 22
consignment, buying on, 32

Declaration of Independence, 25
department store, 90–92
dogs, 76–77
doll house, 39–40
drugstore, 86–89
dry cleaning store, 50–52

escalators, 90
eye doctor, 78, 83
eyeglasses, 78–82

FBI wanted lists, 25
Federal Reserve Bank, 29

film developing, 57–59
films, *see* movies
flowers, 30–31
food: amount bought in supermarket, 19; bread, 5; cake, 5; ice cream, 69–71; soda, 69; spaghetti and meatballs, 6–10; served in restaurant, 6–10, 92; *see also* groceries
frames: eyeglass, 79, 80, 82; picture, 35
furniture, 38; antique, 39, 41; miniature, 40

gas station, 11–12, 100
gasoline, 11–12
groceries, 4, 19, 21

hair cutting, 16–18, 54, 55
hair setting, 54, 55
hardware, 23, 24
hardware store, 3, 23–24, 100
history of stores, 2
hobby, origin of word, 73
hobby shop, 72–73
housewares, 23, 24

ice cream, 69–71
interest, 28

jewelry, 53

kennels, 76–77
keys, 23

laundromat, 98
lumber, 13
lumber company, 13

mail, 25
meat-processing plants, 19, 20–21
medicine, 86–89
merchandise, ordering: antiques, 41; art, 34; books, 34; clothing, 49; department store, 91–92; drugstore, 86–87; florist, 30; furniture store, 38; hardware, 3; kennels, 76; movie theater, 95; pet shop, 75; restaurant, 6; supermarket, 19–20
millwork, 13
money, 2, 11, 25, 26, 27, 28, 84–85, 86, 100; *see also* banks; checks and checking accounts
movies, 94–95

newsstand, 11
night depository, 86

opticians, 78–82

paint, 14–15
pet store, 74–75; *see also* kennels
pets, 74–77
pharmacy, *see* drugstore
phonograph records, 36–37
photographs, 56–59
picture frames, 35
pictures: art prints, 34;
   photographs, 56–59
plants, 30, 31
post office, 25
postage stamps, 25
prescriptions, 86–89
price tags, 91
prints, art, 34
profits, 2, 22, 28
puppies, 76–77

records, *see* phonograph records
rent, store, 2
restaurant, 6–8, 92, 100
robbery, protection against, 26–27

safe-deposit boxes, 27
safes, 27
sales slips, 22

scanner, electronic, 22
service station, *see* gas station
shoes, 42–43; repairing of, 44–47
shoplifting, 48–49
soda, 69
spaghetti and meatballs, 6–10
supermarket, 2, 4, 19–22, 100

theft, protection against:
   in bank, 26–27;
   in clothing store, 48–49;
   in laundromat, 98
trains, miniature, 72–73
trucks, 19, 20

ushers, 95

vaults, 27
vision, 78, 83; *see also* eyeglasses

warehouses: furniture, 38;
   supermarket, 19
washing machines, 98

WITHDRAWN